Aspire for Abundance

Conversations With My Teenage Daughter.

Road Trip Through **Iceland**.

By

Robert N. Jacobs

Grosvenor House
Publishing Limited

All rights reserved
Copyright © Robert N. Jacobs, 2022

The right of Robert N. Jacobs to be identified as the author of this
work has been asserted in accordance with Section 78
of the Copyright, Designs and Patents Act 1988

The book cover is copyright to Robert N. Jacobs

This book is published by
Grosvenor House Publishing Ltd
Link House
140 The Broadway, Tolworth, Surrey, KT6 7HT.
www.grosvenorhousepublishing.co.uk

This book is sold subject to the conditions that it shall not, by way of
trade or otherwise, be lent, resold, hired out or otherwise circulated
without the author's or publisher's prior consent in any form of binding or
cover other than that in which it is published and
without a similar condition including this condition being imposed
on the subsequent purchaser.

This book is a work of fiction. Any resemblance to
people or events, past or present, is purely coincidental.

A CIP record for this book
is available from the British Library

ISBN 978-1-80381-021-8

Acknowledgements

To my beautiful wife – you are truly my better half.
I love you!

To my parents and siblings – in the words of Tina,
"You're simply the best." I love you.

To Ava – this book is for you.
Always be curious! Always stay your authentic self!
Always aspire for abundance.
We love you!

To Ava

*"Always live to your fullest potential
and never settle into a life of stagnation.
If you aspire for abundance in all you do,
you will have an awesome life."*

Dad.

A letter to Ava

Hello Ava

I have never been to Iceland. So, you are already ahead of me.

Your dad and I are different individuals, as are you. I believe we have grown to be good friends because we genuinely appreciate our differences. These differences rest upon a foundation of some core shared values like the integrity at the heart of a hard day's graft, the opportunity inherent in always trying to do your best, the humanity we display by choosing kindness over blame, and the joy we engage when willing others on to success. But we think differently. We act differently. We see the world differently. I know he would love the same relationship with you; for you to become your true self and to pick from these pages the thoughts and observations that truly resonate with you. Your choices. Your energy. Your life.

It turns out that it is what we choose to believe which shapes who we become, something which is echoed in so much of the good advice in these pages. I wish I had understood this when I was your age. This is your dad's gift to you, the chance to pause, to think and to question who you are going to become before the chance to do so has passed you by. As Robbie points out, who you are now is history and already baked-in from your past choices, but who you are choosing to become is the moment of life on which everything important now hinges and pivots. I'm reminded of my favourite song lyric from Pink Floyd's Dark Side of the Moon; 'and then one day you find, 10 years have got behind you. No one told you when to run, you missed the starting gun…' Well Ava, this is your starting gun.

You have a unique coach, because your dad is the most relentless seeker of the facts and evidence that underpin and shape his core beliefs of anyone I have ever met. He reads. He summarises. He travels. He writes. He teaches. He goes the extra mile. He locks his beliefs in. He progresses on the road to a deeper understanding of what he believes really matters. His advice is not random nor whimsical, it is heavily researched and actively curated with the purpose of making the most of our brief visit to the planet.

Others, like me are more random and serendipitous. We are too disorganised or perhaps too lazy to prepare, trek and hunt down life's big answers, preferring instead to sit and ponder, and to dance with the key questions and paradoxes as they arise in our lives. There is no right or wrong way to our journey through life, but we all must choose how we travel on that journey, either deliberately or by default. You cannot opt out while still living.

For me, the big questions are conundrums like; Is life an adventure to be enjoyed or a battle to be endured? Is it a competition or a collaboration? Is it about overcoming fear or realising hope? Is it about now, yesterday or tomorrow? Is it about being significant and standing out from the crowd, or about love, connection and being at one with others? Is it about pleasure or meaning? Is it about being right or being popular? Is it about contribution to others or is it really all about me?! Is life about managing scarcity or enjoying abundance? In my experience, at different moments all of the above show up. The good and the ugly. Without the darkness there can be no light. So, while life may be complex, it is not so complicated really. Having the courage and resilience to choose to enjoy navigating the darkness as much as is humanly possible is what separates the Nelson Mandelas from the Donald Trumps. Your life can be a joy. It can be miserable. It can be sunny or stormy. The only constant is how you choose to show up.

The best start in life is surely to be truly loved from the outset. If nothing else, your dad making the effort to curate his thinking and write to you in this way is a deep act of love and hope. Be grateful for this gift of love which is already baked-in. Not everyone is so lucky. Pay it forward. Whenever the opportunity presents itself, choose kindness before levelling blame. Pick laughter over anger. Take your own path, not mine, your dad's or anyone else's.

Being yourself is not as easy as it might first appear. Thankfully for you, feeling loved is the foundation of confidence, and it is the confidence to make choices in line with who you really are which strengthens the self-worth on which your self-esteem ultimately rests.

It is so easy to be blown off course by the influence of others, making the ability to stand guard over the gates of your own mind a critical life skill.

A lot of your dad's advice is designed to build that confidence by expanding your mind, exploring ideas, and challenging you to think more deeply. Travel far and wide in the world and inside your mind. If you manage this, you will discover that we are so infinitesimally small in our importance and ignorant of the vast majority of what there is to know. As Albert Einstein explained in his 'Paradox of Wisdom', the wiser we become, the more we realise how little we know, which is why another of your dad's themes, curiosity is so important. Black and white thinking simply delivers contrast. It is in the detail offered by the ten million colour hues and shades of grey which change in the light where meaning hides. Choosing to think within and to occupy a binary world of black and white full of faux certainty, silly should-do's, daft rules and unrealistic expectations is a world contained within and constricted by fear, and characterised by scarcity. Choosing to dance with the uncertainty imbued within challenging paradoxes, wearing your heart openly on your sleeve and embracing the inevitable darkness encountered en-route, offers an open world of possibilities characterised by abundance.

When the darkness engulfs you as it inevitably will from time to time, remember the words of Gandalf in The Two Towers, Lord of the Rings '**Look to my coming, at first light, on the fifth day**. At dawn, look to the East'. So, when all seems lost and hope is all but extinguished, seek out the light borne of the love in these pages. They have been written to shine a light when you need it most.

Live well Ava. Make a difference. Be the light.

Best of luck.

Alex Pratt JP OBE

Foreword

Hi. My name is Robbie; Robert to my mother for the last 40-odd years whenever I am in trouble, and trust me, even in my 40s, I still manage to get myself into trouble with her. But for everyone else it's Robbie.

Firstly, just to get it out of the way, I have no PhD in Psychology or in any Cognitive Behavioural Studies. Nor do I have a PhD in Philosophy, Politics, Religious Studies, or any other human behaviour qualification that a typical author of this type of book might have. I do have a couple of business degrees, but most importantly of all in terms of authoring this book, I have made life my university. Successfully? Read on and let's find out together.

Oh… one other thing: I am the father of a beautiful daughter. I'd like to help her avoid the many mistakes I've made in my own life. I even hope to help her avoid some she would have made for herself.

Hence this book.

MY STORY

I saw a cartoon once. I don't remember exactly when, it was a long time ago, but it has stayed with me. In it, a man is walking down the street. Could be any street. Could be any man. Could be me. In fact, in many ways, it was me. The man is smiling – as I recall it, he's both smiling and whistling, which is probably not physically possible – and his strut is sending out a clear message that he's a happy man… *"You want to know what a happy man looks like? He looks like this."* Behind him, there is an enormous hand. This huge hand is curled into a fist with a pointing forefinger that is clearly about to be unleashed on this happy and unsuspecting man. It's so huge that you just know it's going to hit him in the back, and when it does, it's going to project him into the middle of next week – meaning into the unknown, unknowable future. You can look at that hand and forefinger any way you like. It's the hand of God. It's fate. It's kismet. But it's also inescapable. It's there for every one of us, and what gives it its strength is that we don't know it's there and we don't know its power.

It was there, waiting for me, and I hadn't a clue it even existed. I had everything in my life sussed out. I knew where I was going, and I knew how I was going to get there. I knew nothing about this hand, curled up and ready to remind me that it existed, but the hand had not forgotten me. And, of all the days to choose, it struck on my wedding day. This would be the day I discovered I had Type 1 diabetes. Not many people can say they had an ambulance for a wedding car, which, if you look at it in a certain light, was pretty cool. I was driven from my wedding breakfast with sirens and flashing lights; the works. Looking back, there's an element of cool, but it was a little scary at the time.

Being diagnosed with T1D changed my life in so many ways. Not only did I begin a routine of injecting myself four times a day with insulin just to stay alive, but I had a lot of learning to do about nutrition and counting carbs, including forgetting about Red Bulls and a few other things besides. Most of all, I learned about that "hand", and how quickly life can change. One day I was getting nervous about my wedding speech, the next I was in hospital with four drips in my arms, being told that with a blood sugar level of 33, I could have gone into a coma if my wife of one hour had not made me get into the ambulance. I had said I was fine; it was just a passing thing; just natural nervousness about giving up the single life at 40, and I just wanted to get on with it. But she has Italian blood, and when it comes to stubbornness, she has me beaten all ways up. As things turned out, that stubbornness saved my life.

T1D is a chronic disease usually associated with adolescents. They told me I was a "special case" – well, it seems my mother was right when she always told me I was her special child growing up. Being diagnosed with T1D gave me a new thirst for knowledge, a drive to be a better me in all I do, and to be constantly learning. It also made me think about what I can still do with this body that I'm in, and how far I can push it, but now in a healthy way. I've always had a passion for travel. I like to see how people live in different places and different cultures. I try never to travel to the same place twice. My goal is to see a new world wonder every year. So far so good. I can still travel, and I do, but not with quite the same freedom as I once did.

SO, WHY THIS BOOK?

I grew up in a loving family that expected good manners and good morals. You showed respect for your elders, and you treated other people the way you'd like to be treated yourself. My parents, married for more than 50 years, always did their best to ensure we had a balanced life with a spiritual foundation, and that has served me well to this day.

Something I haven't mentioned is that I was born and raised in South Africa. I mention it now because South Africans have a special relationship with Australians. In sport, for example, we like to say (and we mean it), "I support two teams: South Africa, and whoever is playing Australia." I bring this up because I want to quote legendary Australian diplomat Sir Les Patterson, aka Barry Humphries. Sir Les said, *"I am not an orator. I am an Australian politician."* I make no comment on the oratorical skills of Australians, politicians or otherwise, but this is the moment to convey that I am not a guru of anything.

Once upon a time, probably only five hundred or so years ago, it was possible for an educated person to know everything that was known. You could be a polymath, knowing everything there was to know about mathematics, history, classical literature, and the continents and what went on in them. It isn't like that anymore. Today, so much is known about almost everything that if you want to be an expert in anything, you have to abandon all other studies and focus on just that one narrow field. That is not what I want to do. My objective in life is to know a bit about a lot of things, not a lot about one specific thing. Specialising in a specific area is not for me.

When I decided to write this book, I set out to write a personal mission statement declaring my aims. I've been working on it for a while now, and this is what I have so far:

"I aim to ___"

I know I aim to do something. I'm less sure about what it is. Or, I'm quite sure, because I aim to be what is important to me every day, but I also aim to be what is important at any given moment. My aim might be to be grateful for waking up to another beautiful day; to be contributing to a stranger's life; to be a great father, husband, person. The same aims come up every day, but so do completely new things. What I know I want every day is a challenge of some sort that allows me to dedicate my life to learning, to go to bed a little wiser than when I woke up, to never retire, to stay a student of life, and to always stay curious.

My diagnosis has made me focus on my *ikigai*. If this word is unfamiliar to you, it's a Japanese term that sums up the reason you're here. It's what gives your life meaning; a purpose you can work towards, giving you a sense of satisfaction and the feeling that your life makes sense and has a meaning. I plan to still be travelling the world and running marathons with my great-grandkids when I'm celebrating my centenary – but I now appreciate more than ever how quickly life can change. Even with the best strategies in place, the future is promised to no-one.

Like any other father, what I want is the best for my child. The purpose of this book is to help my teenage daughter have an abundant life. A go-to guide to inspire her to soar and explore; to encourage her to be curious and stay authentic; and to motivate her to have high standards in all she does and to only ever settle when she knows she has done her very best. In these pages, I introduce topics that I believe will help her live an abundant life, presenting them as a guide for times when her parents might not be around, for whatever reason, to offer support and guidance in person.

The aim of this book is not to see how many sales I get. That's just vanity. If the contents help even one other person beyond my daughter to think or do something in a more positive way than before, that would be awesome. I want positivity to be an everyday habit, but I believe that for something to become a habit, you need to be reminded of it constantly. You need to think of it constantly and do it constantly, so I'd like to invite all readers to make a habit of grabbing this book whenever they're stuck with one of life's many obstacles.

Also, just to mention; as a Christian father, I have aspirations for my daughter to live a God-fearing life and, therefore, I do go into some depth as to why I see that as important in Chapter 7 – The Platinum Rule. If religion is not your cup of tea, I suggest you pass over this chapter. However, what have you really got to lose? It can only strengthen your own current belief, or – and that's my hope – it can plant a seed and make you curious for some further self-study.

I would also encourage any feedback that you might have, and this can be posted to: feedback@aspireforabundance.co.uk

Our best days are still ahead.

Have fun!

Robert Jacobs
Curious By Design

Table of Content

1. Our Journey Is About to Begin ... 1
2. Iceland: Land of Fire and Ice ... 7
3. Your Journey to Happiness ... 46
4. Build Powerful Habits ... 77
5. Your Tribe Is Your Vibe ... 105
6. Let the World Be Your Playground ... 134
7. The Platinum Rule ... 150
8. Living an Abundant Life ... 165

Iceland: Land of Fire & Ice

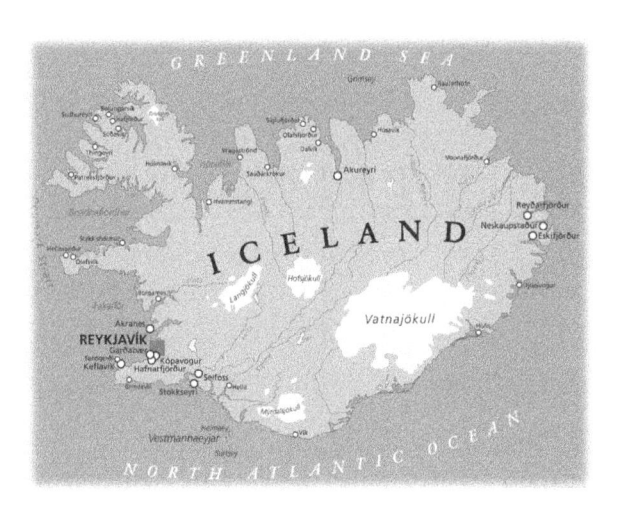

Chapter 1
Our Journey Is About to Begin

*"Abundance is about being rich,
with or without money."* – Suze Orman

Winston Churchill once said, "My most brilliant achievement was my ability to be able to persuade my wife to marry me." Had he been alive today, I would have surely high-fived him and said, "Me too!"

My beautiful wife Simona must surely be one of only a few females on the planet who can not only boast about saving her husband's life, but also doing it on her wedding day. One hour after I said my "I do's", my blood sugar was at 33 – so high that I would have ended up comatose, if not for my wife of one hour phoning 999 and forcing me into the ambulance. (Normal blood sugar levels are around 4.0 to 7.0 mmol/L, not 33!) Having an ambulance for a wedding car was not my first choice, but then with my first choice I would not have been able to ask for the sirens to be put on, weaving through gridlocked traffic – every cloud has a silver lining.

Just like that day, this Iceland trip with my daughter would have remained one more item on my To Do list had Simona not suggested that father and daughter spend some quality time ALONE. We had Ava quite late in life. Simona and I were both in our 40s and, being quite comfortable in my ways, I was not completely convinced that becoming a father was in my future. But Simona has strong Italian blood in her veins and willpower only a Gallotta can have, so I owe to her the ecstasy of holding my own flesh and blood for the first time, wrapped in a fluffy towel, pink and screaming as only a Jacobs could.

We named her Ava Aurora Skye Jacobs. I have always been obsessed with the Aurora Borealis. Why this should be, when I grew up in a small town in South Africa, I have no idea. Maybe it's the obsession with what you can't have, seeing that South Africa is blessed with so much natural beauty itself. Maybe it's the African warmth I grew up with that caused the colder nations to attract me, I don't know. But what I do know is that Iceland was my first foreign trip after I moved to England in the late 90s, and that fascination and love for Iceland and the Northern Lights stayed with me. Knowing she'd need to be able to write her name on her first day at school, we chose Ava as her first name to make it slightly easier for her.

Travelling has always been a big part of Ava's life. When she was three years old, I remember there was an article in a magazine listing all the countries that Prince George had been to during his first three years. I remember noting that Ava had already been to more. Simona and I wanted to bring Ava up knowing that the world is her playground.

I have always said that if I phoned Ava as an adult to ask how she's doing and where she is, I wouldn't want her answer to be "at home" or "at a friend's house"; I'd want it to be somewhere like a quaint coffee shop in Cusco, Papeete, or Ushuaia, where she's enjoying a drink out on the pavement. I want Ava to live an open border life, experiencing and appreciating everything God created on this beautiful planet.

For me, travelling is the best education a person can get. To experience first-hand different cultures, different food, different creation – that is life. It's gaining an early understanding of how different we are as humans, but also how alike we are. Travelling teaches you gratitude and humility. More importantly, it shows you that almost everyone is good and friendly, and in the same way that you do, they just want to get on in life and live in peace – quite different to the impression of the world which watching the news or listening to world leaders motivated by greed, power, and manipulation might give.

Simona and I have always said that we have our best and our worst moments with Ava. When she says, "I love you, Papa" out of the blue and wants a big hug and kiss, that's a best moment. Then when she's not getting her way in public, that's a worst moment. We'd be left trying to save face while the world stared at us and the child with a decibel count that could have challenged the most renowned tenors.

At the age of three, and on a packed flight back from Croatia, everyone heard her repeatedly saying, "Mama, you should not pinch little people." Those pinches were in fact squeezes being given by Simona in a mother's desperate attempt to control her daughter after every other socially acceptable method of discipline had failed. This was followed by another outburst of,

"Papa, you should not use ugly words," after I said something through gritted teeth and with glaring eyes. And then, just like that, as if at the flick of a switch, she'd once more be the angel we knew her to be – most of the time. Now, at the age of 14, she's no longer a little girl, but that little girl is still there inside her.

Age 14 is an interesting time in a girl's life. Girls mature faster than boys, and while bodies change and hormones rage, the ability to rationalise and cope diminishes. At 14, Ava is no longer "Papa's little girl", and what Simona and I thought of as normal is gone. Her mind must tell that her that she is ready for anything. Her actions, however, tell her mother and me a different story. This is an age that challenges even the most compassionate soul. Regardless of when you grew up, 14 is the age when you've never felt more outside yourself, more different, more alone. We've all been there, we've all felt it, and we've all made it to the other side. The truth is, being 14 sucks, and yet it's also one of the most fantastic times of your life. There's no-one on earth smarter than a 14-year-old. With full conviction, you are always right and can't comprehend how undeniably stupid everyone else is, particularly adults, and especially parents. At 14, you might also be wondering why everything you do is wrong, and feeling the world is against you at almost every turn. You're late; you're too slow; you're too loud, and you're too messy... can't you do anything right?

At 14, your social status is of the highest priority, no matter who you leave behind. Your parents are no longer your universe. All that matters is to see your friends and know your place within their circles. It's a jungle out there, and you must fight to be Jane. You eat your parents out of house and home and you start growing up, and sometimes out, and you come to the realisation that some kids can eat without consequence and some just can't – but you still eat because, well, you must. At 14 you're just too cool for school. Teachers, projects, and homework no longer make the grade. School is to friends as chips are to dip. It's just a vessel to get to the good stuff. From the bus ride to the cafeteria, group projects, and sports, peers are priority *numero uno*, and will be until after university at the very least.

Worryingly for your parents, 14 is also that awkward phase where the opposite sex not only suddenly exists, but… *oh là là*! Bodies start responding and things just get weird. At 14, gone are the days of "rise and shine", your bedroom now becoming a dungeon of sheets and sweat. If you are at home without friends, you're in your cave sleeping the day away and dreaming about – actually, I don't want to go there. Your music begins to define who you are and where you are in your life. You listen to and really feel the lyrics, and somehow channel the inner artist in you. You relate to the story being told by the song and sometimes take it on as your own. We know that, because it was the same when we were 14, but there's no point telling you that. Parents don't get it. And then there's the clothes. The girl who once wore nothing but pink takes a walk on the wild side to the war cries of classic rock. Overnight, or so it feels, labelled outfits and dark make-up replace the princess dresses.

At 14, your friends tell you all the things your parents did not want you to know, and anyone who imagines you're not thinking about them is fooling themselves. All we can do, as those who watch over you, is to hope it stays at thinking. In the end, it all comes down to love. I am told that both teenagers and parents of teenagers come out best on the other side of 14 when we have all shown love. As adults, we have all been there, and although our 14-year-olds think they can do anything, they do not have to do it alone – and that's the main reason for our trip together to Iceland. Our journey is about to begin.

Chapter 2
Iceland: Land of Fire and Ice

"Abundance is the ability to do what you need to do when you need to do it." – Bashar

Day 1: London to Reykjavik

Ready for the adventure of a lifetime? Welcome to Iceland. One of Europe's most magical and unforgettable spots, Iceland is the ultimate road trip destination, and it's the road trip Ava and I are about to do as we embark on an adventure that will take us around Iceland in seven days.

As a youngster growing up in sunny South Africa, I was always fascinated by Iceland. I've visited many times, and I absolutely love the country with its dramatic landscapes and stunning natural beauty. It's home to gorgeous glacier lagoons, wild waterfalls, and healing hot springs, and to me it's one of the most magical places on earth. The time of year you visit can make a significant difference. There are very few trees, meaning spring and autumn don't make themselves felt, so Iceland has only two real seasons: summer and winter. Winter slowly turns to summer and summer slowly turns to winter. If it isn't about forests, what is Iceland about? It's possible that others see it differently, but for me, Iceland has dramatic rocky landscapes that make you feel like Neil Armstrong when he first landed on the moon. I remember well the billboard that welcomed me on my first visit in 1999. It read, "Welcome to the Moon", and although there may not have been a "one small step for man, one giant leap for mankind" moment, my first trip to Iceland did not disappoint.

It doesn't matter what kind of traveller you are, Iceland caters for you. If you're an adventure seeker, you can hike through ice caves and climb glaciers. If you're a photographer, you will be blown away by the landscapes and waterfalls. Outdoorsy people will love camping around the Ring Road and the lesser-known hidden gems, and if all you want is to relax, Iceland offers amazing geothermal pools and spas. I've always maintained that I would never travel to the same place twice – there are too many other places to see and people to know – but Iceland has been the exception. Why? There are so many reasons, but in a nutshell, this is where Mother Nature spends most of her time, happily showing off her diversity in a vast technicolour range. Nature and beauty are everywhere, and I'm also always surprised by how modern, yet traditional Iceland is, and all of this just below the Arctic Circle.

Here we are, with months of planning behind us, the time is here, and Ava and I are visiting this wondrous place again. Our previous visits have all been in the lighter months when the Earth's summertime tilt means somewhere as far north as Iceland gets up to 22 hours of sunshine and temperatures range from a cool 10 degrees to a very comfortable 15-plus degrees in July. This time will be our first trip in December. Something else we're doing for the first time on this trip is venturing far outside the Reykjavik peninsula for a seven-day tour around the Icelandic Ring Road, a.k.a. Route 1. This is kind of like the M25 around London, except that in this case it circumnavigates the whole country. We've been told there's no better way to explore Iceland, and at 828 miles (1332 km) long, people say it's among the world's top road trips. We are about to find out.

Temperatures around zero degrees, and only a couple of hours of sunlight each day, are not the only things on this trip that will test both of us. We'll be spending a lot of time together in the car and hotels. My patience is going to be tested dealing with my 14-year-old know-it-all daughter on our first trip without her mother. Hers too will undoubtedly be tested by her 50-something father who still thinks he's cool doing his MC Hammer *Can't Touch This* moves to every song on her playlist. I'm not setting out to embarrass her, but who knows what might happen when the long hours of darkness begin to weigh on us.

Where It All Began

Growing up in a small town in South Africa, thinking and playing big – or what I now perceive to be thinking big – was not what most people did. I grew up in a happy home with my three siblings and loving parents, and it wasn't until I was 19 that I boarded my first plane. That first flight was an hour long and took me from Johannesburg to Durban. Two years later, at the age of 21, I was invited to a party by a new university friend and found myself for the first time inside what people would still describe today as a mansion. Driving through the neighbourhood to my friend's house,

I couldn't stop staring at the houses we drove past. He lived in a house that was bigger than anything I'd ever seen – the house, the swimming pool, the cars, even the dog seemed massive.

For 21 years I'd lived less than 20 miles from this neighbourhood and never knew it was there, or at least I knew it only as something seen from a distance driving past on the motorway. For 21 years, I'd lived in a world that was familiar to me. Our neighbours were just like us. My friends in school were just like me. We were middle-class, or so I thought. Kids with fathers who worked hard for a boss, and mothers who mostly stayed at home working just as hard raising their children. What I didn't know then, but know now, is that middle-class is such a broad term. This all came home to me when my "rich" friend told me that they considered themselves middle-class. If they were middle-class, what were we?

At 24, I decided to step outside my comfort zone, and my first big decision was to move to England. It was only going to be for a couple of years. Some 30 years later, I'm still here. England is an amazing country to live in, and I thank my parents often for sacrificing so much and giving me the opportunity to spread my wings. Fresh out of college and streetwise from studying in a city like Johannesburg, I was confident that I could handle everything life threw at me. My brother and I were the first I knew of among our friends and family to venture outside the borders of South Africa for anything more than a short holiday. This was a big step for us.

I landed in London on the 19th of January, 1999. That's high summer in South Africa, and I hadn't done my research, because I was wearing a T-shirt and shorts. I remember how cold it was that day, and I remember thinking on the train from Heathrow to London how small the houses next to the tracks were and how on top of each other people lived. I also noticed how grey it was, and how no-one on the train smiled. *Welcome to your new life,* I thought.

My mental image of England was of men being gentlemen who played cricket and women being ladies who did high tea. I was therefore in for a quick reality check, but one thing I was determined not to do was make quick use of my return ticket to South Africa, even if I had to sleep on a park bench. Determination, or my ego? I still don't know. All I know is that I had left a place where dirty laundry disappeared from the corner of my room and magically reappeared the next morning in my closet, cleaned, ironed, and folded; a place where food magically appeared on the table every time my mother said, "Dinner is ready", and I'd arrived in a place where life simply wasn't like that. But this was going to be my new life for now, and I was going to see it through. The seeds for travelling and experiencing new things were planted.

Within a few hours of landing in London, I was at an employment agency, and later that evening started my first job in my new country. I worked the night shift, 11pm to 7am, for a haulage company. Lorries packed with parcels came in, and the parcels had to be offloaded and then loaded onto other lorries. I had just finished my master's degree and my professors might have wondered what the point of my studies had been, but the exchange rate meant the rands I had brought with me wouldn't last long and I needed to start earning pounds. I can still feel the cold wind blowing through the open warehouse doors, and I was wearing loads of T-shirts to keep me warm. During my shift, there were a few short breaks between unloading one lorry and loading another. The team would try to get a quick power nap in a heated Portakabin. I was so intimidated by the other guys with their tattoos and weird accents that I gained an understanding of what "sleeping with one eye open" really meant. As it was, this would be a valuable lesson in not judging a book by its cover. These were the good guys, trying to make a living in a country where they could easily have been on benefits and received a handout that wouldn't have been much less than their wages.

After three months, I found something a bit more in my field and with more sociable hours. It was tough going, but I think back fondly on those times. Years of working seven-day weeks, sleeping on blow-up mattresses, and rationing the slices of ham for my sandwiches. Saving every penny I earned, I never lost track of the bigger picture. My original plan had been to stay in the UK for two years, work, do a bit of travelling, and save. I'd then go back to what I still thought of as home. Property in South Africa at that time was much cheaper than now, and an exchange rate of 20 rand to the pound meant I would be able to buy and pay for my first house in South Africa in two years. But, as John Lennon once said, "Life is what happens while you're busy making other plans", and for the last 30 years, I haven't been back to South Africa for more than a holiday. However, what I learned at the time was that if I worked hard enough, I could have the things I wanted: security, and a house of my own.

I learned something else. In South Africa, I'd had this dream of one day visiting Iceland. Jo'burg to Reykjavík is 7100 miles. But I was in London, which meant I'd already knocked off 6000 of those miles. Could there be a better time to make my first visit to Iceland? I couldn't think of one, so in true "if not now, when?" spirit, I got on a plane. In some ways, it felt like paying off another mortgage, because Iceland is not a destination for travel on a shoestring, but that trip was for me the beginning of travelling as often and as much as possible.

Early Morning Realisations

The night before embarking on the trip to Iceland with Ava, I'd struggled to get to sleep. I lay staring at the ceiling, glimpsing 12.51am on the digital clock. I've always been a night owl, but rising nerves about our upcoming trip were adding to the difficulty in getting to sleep. Simona knew this, but she had been encouraging me to get some shut-eye as the flight was early, at 6.30am, and she wanted an awake and alert man taking care of her daughter, not a zombie.

Thanks to Simona's insistence, I managed to get an hour's rest, but falling completely asleep was impossible.

My mind had set off into some of the most bizarre scenarios that could happen while we were away. It seemed as though the fates were trying to tell me that this trip was not a good idea. Not for the first time, I wished I hadn't given in to Simona's wishes, and I still hoped that she would change her mind and surprise us by joining us on our trip. However, the trip was planned, and I knew deep down that hoping such a thing was futile. Sleep remained elusive, and after twisting and turning and grappling with irrational thoughts, I gave up trying. Where were these thoughts coming from? Finally, the root of my worries dawned on me. I was going on a trip with Ava, and there were so many things I didn't know about her. Who are her friends? Is she having trouble at school, or in her studies? What are her dreams for the future?

We were going to be together, just the two of us, and maybe I'd developed a subconscious fear about what we'd have to talk about. Many fathers may respond by saying, "What's the big deal? Fathers aren't supposed to know much about their daughters. That's a mother's job." But for me it was a big deal, because the distance between us had not always been there. In her early years, Ava and I had a very close relationship. I don't think I flatter myself when I say she saw me as the coolest person in her life. But time brought changes. That's the irritating thing about time; you think you've got everything the way you want it, and then the universe says, "Okay, Mr Smart Guy, let's see what you make of this." I went from being the person with whom Ava shared everything to being the last person to hear anything.

I'm not going to say that women understand relationships better than men do, because I'm sure there are huge numbers of men who will say, "Not in my case, Buster." And, in fact, I know that there are women who make an unholy mess of every relationship in their lives, so I restrict myself to saying that Simona understands human relationships a great deal better than I do. I don't think my experience is unusual. There are plenty of "daddy's girls" who begin to gravitate more towards their mothers as they start their journey into womanhood. Yes, it was disappointing for me to lose the coolest person title, but that didn't mean that Ava and I had to grow completely apart. Our relationship would be different – it *had* to be different – but it could still be important. Simona knew this and, being the wise woman she is, she suggested that Ava and I should spend time together, without her, a thousand miles away. It was a suggestion that had an instant effect, as simply planning the itinerary for our Iceland trip was the closest Ava and I had been for some time.

When the alarm went off, it was dark and wintry outside, and I made my way down to the kitchen. Ava was already dressed, bags by the door, and eating her Weetabix while leaning against the kitchen table.

'Coffee, Dad?'

'A strong one, please,' was my reply. I needed a boost after a bad night's rest.

I finished loading the car with what looked like enough bags for a year-long excursion. Ava said her goodbyes to Simona and went to sit in the car. Simona and I hugged each other goodbye and, still in embrace, she murmured in my ear, "Have a great time and show Ava what she is missing by not having her father as a best friend. It's high time my husband won back the coolest guy title."

Iceland This Way!

We arrived at Keflavik airport just after 9am. When you look at a map, Iceland seems so far west of the UK that it's always a surprise to find that they are in the same time zone. As we walked to the luggage carousel, we were greeted by a billboard showing a woman in the rain standing in the Blue Lagoon. The headline on the billboard read, "Iceland, this way". After months of planning, we were here at last.

Our initial plan had been to visit the Blue Lagoon first before heading to Reykjavik, but I had left it till the last minute to make reservations, meaning we couldn't get in until six in the evening. As it happened, the nine-hour wait was a good thing, because the lagoon was much less crowded later in the day. Most flights to Iceland arrive first thing in the morning, and everyone heads straight to the Blue Lagoon since it's close to the airport.

It was cold, but the sky was blue, and the sun was shining. Who ever said Decembers in Iceland are not for the faint-hearted? We collected our car and embarked on the hour-long journey from Keflavik to the capital. Reykjavík is a small and artsy city, buzzing with activities, sprinkled with Scandinavian huts and a cluster of bars and museums. Some of my favourite spots in the city are the Old Harbour with its cool cafes, the Sun Voyager boat sculpture, and Hallgrímskirkja church, where an excellent view of the city can be had from the top. We also managed to get some hot dogs at Bæjarins Beztu Pylsur (try saying that out loud), Iceland's famous hot dog stand.

Although Reykjavik is the capital of Iceland and the largest city in the country, it is still relatively small and can be seen within a day or two. We checked into our Airbnb at around 3pm and enjoyed our lovely apartment for a bit before heading off to the Blue Lagoon for early dinner and relaxation. We had a 5pm reservation at LAVA, giving us an hour to eat before our 6pm reservation at the lagoon.

LAVA's dining room is awesome; it's like being in a luxury cave, with huge windows looking out to the lagoon. We ordered the lamb and ribeye, and everything was fantastic! While waiting for our desserts, I asked Ava what she would like to get from the trip, and what would make it a successful trip in her mind. Her quick response was seeing the Northern Lights, and I naturally agreed, but it gave me an opportunity to point out that there was no guarantee of seeing the lights and to ask if not seeing them would mean the trip was a failure.

Ava wasn't sure of the answer to that, so she turned the tables by asking what would make this trip a success for me. Here was my chance to tell her about what I really wanted out of this trip. I told her that, for me, success would be catching up: talking about things that might be worrying her; things that might be worrying me; and how things were going in school. Effectively, a bit of old-fashioned dad-daughter bonding, and maybe a way for me to understand more about her dreams for the future. After that, success would be taking her home safely to her mother.

"You don't need to worry about any of that, Dad. Everything is going fine," was her response.

Was that supposed to make me feel better? Somehow it didn't, because the word "fine" has at times been code for something far from fine when used by Simona, and an indicator that I should watch out! Well, time would tell.

What Is Success to You?

With the bill paid, we went to our locker rooms and changed into our bathing suits. It was pretty cold by now, and my 10-yard dash to the lagoon would have left Usain Bolt feeling proud. Slowly walking through the warm water was a bittersweet sort of feeling; my body enjoyed the heat, but my bald head was less keen on the ice crystals landing on it. However, it was here that the first sign of getting my wish for greater closeness began to appear. As we strolled through the shoulder-depth water, our feet sinking into the sludge underneath, Ava began to talk about success.

"I hear a lot from my friends about wanting to be successful when they grow up, success is clearly a goal for them, but what they mean by success is less clear.

How do you know if you are successful? What is success?" she asked.

This was exactly the kind of conversation I'd wanted, so I jumped right in. "My view on that might be different to your friends," I answered, "because I don't see success as an end goal. Success is what follows a positive action. Success is a victory along the road of life, and it can be a small victory."

"If I become rich, drive a nice car, and have a big house, will that be success?" was her response.

I replied with, "Yes, it will. *If* you are also happy. Those things – the money, the big house, the posh car – that's how the material world today sees success, but there's an assumption built into that assessment, and it's that those things bring happiness. They don't. The world is full of rich people who look very happy on the surface and come across as successful, by worldly standards, but deep down they feel they lack something. Some appear to have everything, but suffer from depression. Some go through ugly divorces, and some, despite outward appearances, end up taking their own lives."

I looked at her, unsure whether to go on, but she looked as though she was listening, so I added, "Real success isn't about the possessions you have. It's a state of mind. It's happiness, and happiness is not what you have, it's who you are. It comes from taking actions every day, no matter how small, to better your life in some way, so that you are in a better position tomorrow." I then asked, "Would you regard Mother Teresa and Gandhi as success stories?" Her nod was emphatic. Yes, it seems she certainly would. This gave me the go ahead to say, "And did you know that the only possessions they had were the things they carried with them? Things small enough to fit into a bag they could carry?"

Ava was thoughtful for a moment, then asked, "So, how do I judge whether *I'm* being successful?"

"You mean now, as a 14-year-old?" I queried. "Well, what qualifies as success varies depending on your stage of life, so for you, right now, success might be being more prepared for your history test, meaning you're in a good position to improve on your last grade. Or, it might be saving your pocket money instead of spending it on things you don't really need, meaning you have the funds to buy a ticket to the concert you really want to go to. Or, for a runner like you, it might be getting your 5km time down...'

At this point, I thought about what I'd just been saying and realised that what I'd really been doing was thinking out loud. "What is success?" was a question I was trying to answer for my own benefit as well as Ava's. Having stopped to think, I was then able to say, "Success does not need to be major achievements; it hardly ever is. Success is always taking one more small step forward. Progress is our most important goal."

She then said, "Dad, would you consider yourself successful?"

This threw me a little, but this was also the daughter I'd always known – never afraid to ask a direct question.

"Well," I answered, "if I go by how I defined success when I was around your age, the answer will have to be no. Back then, I had a poster of a red Ferrari on one wall and a green Kawasaki Ninja motorcycle on another. I would lie in bed with big dreams of driving those two monsters. That's what I thought of as success, and I thought owning them would let me know I was successful."

It was strange to think back, but it was true. After the Ferrari phase, I'd moved into a yellow BMW M3 phase, with success being me driving around wearing my Don Johnson *Miami Vice* suit and white pointed shoes. At one point in my life, I did have the suit and the shoes, but never the BMW. I had thought that I'd know what it was to be successful when I was driving along with the window down, my elbow resting on the door panel, and the bass pumping out from speakers so massive that I'd had to convert the car boot to house the booster. Perhaps I would have felt successful, but it would only have been for a while. "If I'd owned those things, any success I felt wouldn't have lasted," I said, "because what I know now, and maybe it took me too long to realise, is that success and happiness are not end results.

"Owning this or that isn't being successful; success is a feeling. What you have isn't important; it's who you are and who you are becoming as you work towards achieving your goals. Once you have a goal, success is your daily journey towards it, no matter how slow it might feel for you. What I'm trying to say is that instead of seeing yourself as the person you are now, see yourself as the person you will become. You might even think of it as being like your swimming coach always telling you to visualise your race before you even enter the water. You see, the same goes for success. Visualise already having what you want and being who you want to be. Visualising is a very important part of reaching your goals."

Of course, Ava being my smart daughter, there was an obvious question about to arise from what I'd just said. "But what if I'm not sure what to visualise right now, Dad? What if what I visualise now turns out not to be what I want to visualise in a few years' time? Like you and the Kawasaki?"

This was, of course, a good question! At 14, you have your whole life ahead of you. In my answer, I explained that there's nothing wrong with changing your mind as your interests in life change, and switching from one dream to another is to be expected. Lots of people change their career later in life, and there are plenty of people who start new hobbies or sports or discover new interests and creative talents throughout their lives. I was 42 before I ran my first marathon, having never really been much into running before then. Now, I've taken part in marathons on six continents and at the North Pole. This meant that the best advice I could give, and to give an answer to her question, was simply to keep trying new things and not get bogged down, especially at the age of 14, with trying to find *one* path through life.

Although active in sports, it was fair to say that Ava had become a bit of a social media slave. When you're 14, you're standing with your peer group is of such vital importance that you can't understand or imagine that this will tail off as you grow older. I had to tread carefully on this topic, but I had something I needed to say.

"Ava, I wonder if spending quite the amount of time you spend scrolling and texting is really the best use of time? Your mother and I understand the importance of healthy social experiences, but I can't help thinking that if you halved the time you spend on social media and used the extra time to read a book, plan another adventure, or learn a new skill like the cooking class you did with your mother last month, you might find life a lot more meaningful and fun."

"Are you saying I spend too much time on social media?"

"Noooo... I'm saying that life is not a dress rehearsal. You don't get another chance at it. So, you have to spend your time wisely, and that means focusing on developing yourself. Try a lot of things until you find that one thing that you have a passion for – and you can still leave time for your friends on social media as well."

"Isn't thinking about myself in that way a bit selfish, Dad? You always say that the biggest joy in life comes from helping and giving to people who are less fortunate than us."

"It might sound selfish, but believe me, it isn't. Remember the announcement on the flight coming over to Iceland where they said that in case of an emergency, oxygen masks will drop from above and to please make sure that you attend to yourself first before you attend to others? They say that because it's not going to be possible to help others without looking after yourself first. If the cabin pressure on a plane flying at 35,000 feet drops, it only takes about 20 seconds for the passengers to lose consciousness. Of course, the natural reaction for any parent would be to get the mask onto their children first, but if they haven't put their own mask on first, they're in danger of losing consciousness when those 20 seconds are up – and then they can't help anyone. It's looking after themselves first that allows them to look after others."

This had clearly given Ava some food for thought, so I felt I needed to find a way to justify my comment. "You're right in that ultimate success in life is all about making the lives of others better and contributing positively to your community. But you can only do that if you are coming from a position of mental strength yourself. No-one takes a lot of notice of what you tell them. It's what you *show* them that makes the difference. Telling others that they should spend less time on social media is not going to hold any water if you are constantly on social media yourself; telling others that they should eat a healthier diet doesn't cut it if you're constantly grazing on junk food yourself. To inspire people to make changes for the better, you need to show them what making those changes looks like – you need to be a positive example of the benefits. This is really what looking after yourself and striving to be your best self is all about; it's not selfishness. There is no greater feeling than knowing that someone is in a better state today because of your inspiration and guidance, and the positive example you gave the day before. When this happens, you feel successful, no matter what your age or dreams in life."

I went on to explain that success is not something you can achieve by chasing it, it's something you attract by being your best self. If you keep working on improving yourself, and putting your energy into being a better you, the rest will fall into place. I wish I'd known all these things when I was Ava's age. Schools teach all sorts of stuff that most of us forget as soon as we leave, and life skills never seem to be on the curriculum. Of course, this doesn't mean that school lessons serve no purpose; learning is important, and learning should be a lifelong habit for all of us. It's often said that learners are earners, and continuing to work on self-development once your school days are over is just as important as career development. It's human nature to always be striving, but you do have a choice over what you're striving for.

Sadly, many people fall into the trap of striving for more stuff they don't need: more money, more possessions, and often getting into more debt just to keep up with the Joneses. This sort of striving is a quick route to unhappiness and depression. There's nothing wrong with wanting or having nice things, but it's important to understand that possessions can't provide any real or lasting happiness. Real riches are the by-products of doing something you really love. Don't believe people when they say that money is the root of all evil. It's not the money, it's the love of money, and the willingness of some people to put having more of it above all else that's the evil.

For me, success is going to bed at night and sleeping peacefully with no worries over things future or past, and simply dreaming big dreams. I always had big dreams, but since being diagnosed with Type 1 diabetes at the age of 40, I've taken "successes" more seriously. I've also learned that dreams on their own are no use to anyone, you have to do something about them. What I did – and admittedly it took a crisis to make it happen – was to start living a more focussed life and not just dabble with things here and there. That's a lesson I learned, but I wanted Ava to know that it didn't need to be the same for her. There are thousands of people who find their purpose after a crisis, and that's a good thing for them in their lives, but it's even better if you don't need to wait until you're 40 to begin understanding what life is trying to tell you.

Clarity Is Power

"Clarity is power" is something Tony Robbins once said, and I wholeheartedly agree. Something I've learned is that getting what you want out of life begins and ends with being specific about what it is you want. Not everyone knows what that is right away, and that's where trying lots of new things comes in, but to achieve any goal, you need to be able to visualise every tiny detail of it. Research has proven that the human brain is unable to differentiate between visualisation and reality, so if you have a clear vision of what you want, it will soon manifest itself. This may sound like wishful thinking, but visualisation techniques have been used by elite athletes to great effect for many years, and those techniques have been adopted by people in business, education, and by anyone interested in becoming more than they currently are.

To help get my point across, I said, "Never stop working on yourself. Have dreams and goals so big they scare you. Thinking small is not what God wants from you and me. We can all be lions, but we choose to live like mice. We all have great potential; it is all down to clarity in what we want, and taking action."

On the kitchen wall at home, I have a vision board that's full of pictures, quotes, affirmations, and items related to a specific goal or set of goals. It's something I started 15 years ago, and I can honestly say that almost every goal that has featured on my vision board has become a reality. A vision board may be focussed on future events, but I now know that our destinies are shaped by the decisions we take today.

Every step we will ever take will have consequences. Even taking no steps at all is a decision and, like every decision, there are consequences. Every step we have ever taken in the past has led us directly to where we are right now... which for Ava and I was relaxing in the Blue Lagoon with white mud on our faces.

I remembered a time when Ava told me that she would love to study medicine at Oxford University one day, so I used this as an example of getting specific. "If that's something you really want, it can become a great goal to strive for. Once you have made up your mind, you need to break down your goal into smaller more immediate goals. A starting point might be to understand what subjects you need to take and what grades you need to get. Knowing that, you then need to sit down and work out how much time you need to spend each day studying to get the grades required. You could speak to someone already studying medicine at Oxford and see what tips they might have to improve your chances, and you could sign up for newsletters, and get familiar with the curriculum. All of these actions translate to thinking and breathing your goal. The more you think about it, the more the universe will help you to keep taking steps towards it. There's a great Stephen Covey quote that sums this up perfectly: 'Whatever the mind can conceive and believe, it can achieve.' Think big!"

At this point, Ava was keen to point out that going to Oxford wasn't yet a firm ambition; it was just a thought, not a committed decision. This allowed me to explain that it was just a way of demonstrating how to get specific with a goal, and it flagged up the fact that wherever it is you decide you want to go, there's no way of getting there if you don't have the address! The address represents the specifics of your goal. I said, "You remember how we worked out an itinerary of what we want to do and see each day while we're in Iceland? That's what you do – you work out your itinerary. You need to plan, and you write down what a good day will look like; what a good week, and a good month will look like. You set yourself a goal, but if you want to get there, you need a map. A plan. But remember, when sensible people talk about their plan, they also talk about their Plan B.

"We live in a world full of distractions, and unplanned things will always come up, so it's probably impossible to stick to a map 100% of the time. With the best will in the world, not everything on every 'today list' is going to get done, but it's where you start. You focus on what the perfect day ahead might look like for you, and then at the end of that day, you go through your list and note what you did and what you were unable to do. You can then begin to build a picture of why you were unable to get those things done. Perhaps you were just a bit too ambitious, or you simply had too many things on your list. Maybe there was one thing on the list that was so hard to achieve that you just had no time left for anything else. The big task, or the most daunting task, is something Brian Tracy calls your 'frog'. As ugly as it might sound, his advice is that you eat your frog first. What he means by this is that you do the thing you're tempted to put off doing first. Getting it done will give you a huge sense of accomplishment and make the other tasks on your list feel so easy. To begin with, try to achieve at least 50% of what is on your list. As you get more familiar with the system, aim for a higher percentage. Your plan A might be to study at Oxford, but you still need to have a plan B. There is no disgrace in reaching for the stars and landing on the moon."

Having a plan isn't a complete answer to getting to where you want to go, but it's an essential start. To execute your plan, you need to be able to manage distractions, and the world is full of them. Limiting the amount of time spent watching TV and on social media is a good start, and I wanted to encourage Ava to spend more time reading.

"Reading is the key to a successful life, and if you want to be everything you can be, you will need to have read a lot of books. They say that reading is like having a conversation with the author. Imagine having conversations with the greats of the past: Abraham, David, Jesus, Ruth, Socrates, Cicero, Marcus Aurelius, and more recently, Da Vinci, Newton, Tesla, Gandhi, or Mandela. Would having conversations and learning lessons from these people not make you a more enlightened and knowledgeable person? Keep reading as much as possible – always."

Ava agreed and said that she was going to make setting goals and mapping out the way to achieve them her New Year resolution. This was good to hear, but I wasn't sure about letting goals become associated in her mind (or anybody's mind) with New Year resolutions. The problem with New Year resolutions is that they never last, and the statistics relating to January gym memberships are a prime example. It's a fact that 70% of those who join a gym at the beginning of January have stopped going by March. Why wait for a future date or time to set your goals? Why not start right now? There's an old Chinese proverb that makes this point beautifully: The best time to plant a tree was 20 years ago, and the second-best time is now.

This felt like the perfect moment to apply the "in for a penny, in for a pound" approach to life, and I said, "Let's make a goal right now." I reminded her about something we'd noted before when reading about high achievers. They very often seem to be early risers, so I made a suggestion. "Let's decide to wake up at 5 every morning while we're in Iceland. We'll start the day with 20 minutes of exercise, 20 minutes of meditation or reflection, and then 20 minutes of reading. We'll have breakfast by 6, and be out of the door by 7 to make the most of every day." I did think I was probably pushing it with this idea, but to my surprise, Ava agreed. This was to be our standard.

Setting a standard is not the same as setting a goal. In fact, it's not so much setting new goals that brings happiness in life, it's setting higher standards in living. Once you know what you want to do, it's very important to set goals. Let's use getting into medical school as an example. In this case, getting the grades needed would be an essential goal, but standards go beyond goals; they are who you are. Mediocre standards lead to a mediocre life. A person's standards can be seen in the way they present themselves and in their everyday habits and interactions with others. Standards are in appearance, but it's not about vanity, and in a person's morals and the company they choose to keep. It's one of those things that everyone knows without necessarily knowing they know, and standards in life are at the heart of many old sayings – and in jokes. There's a story about a vicar who stops by the immaculate garden of a parishioner. He says, "You and God have worked miracles on this patch of land, Fred." "Yes," says Fred. "But you should have seen it when God had it to himself."

You might say that Fred's goal was to have a garden that others would admire, and without his hardworking standard, the goal would never have been achieved.

The same need for high standards is always evident in the world of competitive sport. Onlookers might comment on a lucky shot or some other "lucky" happening that leads to victory, but the athletes themselves know that success is not down to luck, and as many have said, "The harder I work, the luckier I get." The success of Fred's garden and the wins in sport are down to setting high standards and then committing to putting in the work to achieve them. Plenty of sportspeople might set themselves the goal of winning a major title in their sport, but only a few will ever realise that goal. So what's the difference that makes the difference? Inherited genetic makeup may have a role to play, but having Olympic champion parents doesn't make you a born champion. Good coaching may also be a factor, but not every athlete coached by the same champion coach will make it to the top of their game. The difference is found in the standards each athlete sets for themselves. Those committed to maintaining the highest standards are those who succeed.

When 18-year-old Emma Raducanu became the first ever qualifier to win a major tennis tournament, it left me wondering how many other young up-and-coming players have dreamt of standing on the podium at the US Open and holding the trophy high. I suspect a huge number, yet Emma stands alone in having fulfilled her dream. Why her? Well, there are plenty of theories and opinions, but it seems fair to put it down to the high standards she set for herself, alongside her parents' commitment to helping her achieve those standards. She put in the hours of training before she went to school in the morning, and she trained again after school. When she recognised aspects of her game that could be improved, she sought advice on how to make those improvements. She's not unique in this, but something that demonstrates the high standards she has set for herself in life, not just tennis, is the fact that in the few months between her appearance at Wimbledon and her win in the US Open, she sat her A-levels, achieving an A* in maths and an A in economics. A huge amount of work goes into completing these courses and achieving these grades, and the lesson we can all learn from Emma is that we should always aim to put our best effort into *everything* we do. Always doing your best and being yourself can only ever lead to becoming your best in whatever you choose to do.

I wanted Ava to understand that she should always strive for higher standards, but she also needed to know that this would mean spending time getting to know herself and discovering what she wanted out of life. I could tell her with some certainty that what you think you want at 14 is going to be different to what you want at 40, but even as a 14-year-old, it's important to think about where you'd like life to take you. My advice is to write things down, meditate over your thoughts, and reflect on them often. I am a firm believer that where you put your focus, your energy will flow. Focus on what you want. Be specific, and then spend the energy required to get there. You are not on your own. The universe is not indifferent. That's the great fallacy that holds so many people back. The American poet Stephen Crane wrote:

> A man said to the universe:
> "Sir, I exist!"
> "However," replied the universe,
> "The fact has not created in me
> A sense of obligation."

Crane was doing what poets do; he was using his media of poetry to describe the world as he saw it. He deserves every credit for that, but he was wrong. The energy of the universe will work with your energy in making your goals manifest themselves. But only if you go about it the right way. This is not an occasional exercise to be indulged in when you feel like it and with only the amount of energy you happen to feel like putting into it at the time. The universe will respond to this approach with an attitude of, "Well, if s/he doesn't care all that much about what s/he wants, why should I?" A sense of urgency is needed in terms of what you want, and what you want must become the thing you think of most. Your thoughts become things.

What you want to achieve can't be something you'd "like to do" one day. It needs to be something you "must do" and are prepared to do whatever it takes for as long as it takes to do it. You must be passionate about what you do. You want to be a doctor? Great, but are you sure? Is medicine and helping people really your passion? Most people who are successful in whatever field they have chosen will tell you that they have not worked a day in their lives. They are passionate about what they do and love doing it. Doing what you love no longer feels like work. Of course, it won't always be plain sailing. There are going to be times in life that you have to do what you don't particularly want to do or enjoy doing, but with a clear goal in mind, these times can be understood as steps that must be taken to help you get to where you really want to go.

I could see that Ava had some reservations about these ideas. She pointed out that she dreams of doing many things, but she couldn't think of any that had actually come to pass. This was leading her to question whether a person's level of success was in fact determined by how clever they were. It can seem that way, but there's a difference between dreaming and setting goals and standards. A person is like a magnet. Think big and you will attract other big thinkers, but most people think small, and they attract small thinkers. I got Ava to think about some of the great companies she often talked about – Google, Amazon, Apple, Tesla – and then consider the fact that they are all located within 20 miles of each other. Why? Because like-minded people attract like-minded people. If you want to succeed, you need to spend time with and be around successful people, and avoid spending too much time around low frequency people who have a way of draining your energy and dragging you down. Think big and you will live big. You will live big in happiness, in accomplishments, in income, and in respect. You will stand out by thinking big and taking actions according to your thinking. Success is not determined by your IQ, but by the size of your thinking and your attitude. You need to remind yourself daily that your attitude is far more important than your intelligence.

An Attitude of Success

Your attitude towards life is critical, and attitude starts with thinking. It's not necessarily the brightest people who make it to the top, it's attitude and drive that will get you there. If you are committed to studying medicine, it will be your attitude and drive that will get you to your goal. A certain level of intelligence is going to be needed, of course, but intelligence alone can't get you there if you don't have the drive to keep moving towards it. In sport, talent alone isn't enough to make it to the top of your game, it takes grit and determination to push through all the challenges an athlete will inevitably face along the way. The message I wanted Ava to receive out of all of this is that you need to focus on your attitude in everything you do, and you need to know the "why" of everything you do. When you have the "why", you can find the "how".

Your attitude towards something can be decided in a heartbeat. Ralph Waldo Emerson once said, "If I know what you think, I know who you are." What he meant by this is that our thoughts make us who we are. Our mental attitude is the X factor that determines our fate. Two people can be struck by the same set of unfortunate events and see things entirely differently. One might choose to see it for what it is, a temporary setback from which valuable lessons can be learned and immediate action taken to improve the situation. The other might choose to feel the weight of the world on their shoulders, see life as unfair, slip into why-do-things-always-go-wrong-for-me thinking, take no action whatsoever, and spiral into a dark world of depression, self-pity, and loneliness. The same set of circumstances combined with different attitudes results in very different outcomes.

To put this into a personal context, I reminded Ava of my fear of needles. Needles have always scared me, and they still do, but when I had to start injecting myself with insulin four times a day, I never for one moment slipped into "why me?" thinking. Instead, I praised the guy who discovered insulin, because he had given me the chance to live and not die as so many diabetics had done only a century or so ago. Instead of being depressed, what may have been construed as a negative happening by some gave me the extra oomph I needed to focus on living a positive life in every way and in everything I chose to do.

Ava still wasn't entirely sold. She'd had enough experience of people to know that it wasn't uncommon for some to make fun of other people's goals. This was a serious point she was raising. It's sadly true that not everyone likes to see other people standing out from the crowd. I believe this is because it highlights their own insecurities and attitudes towards life, so if this should happen, my advice to her is to remember that someone who belittles you or the way you're thinking wants everyone to be like them. Average.

"If you're happy with being average, accept it. But I know you're not, so however close to you these people might be, limit your association with them. If that's what it takes, cut them off completely. Being around negative, energy-sapping, complaining people needs to feel uncomfortable, because if it doesn't, you're not going to reach your goals. People who tell you that something can't be done are almost always unsuccessful people, and what they mean is not that it can't be done but that *they* can't do it. It's not their roadmap you need to be following, it's yours. It's your life, and you need to lead it the way that's best for you."

Robin Sharma once said that haters confirm greatness. This is something we should use as a test in life. You need to be very aware of who the haters are. When you really start making waves, the haters will be intimidated by you. They won't see you as a positive example of what they could also achieve; they'll see you negatively because you're highlighting what they're not doing. They won't understand how you're doing what you do, and they'll be afraid of what they don't understand. Yes, people will mock your efforts and try to belittle you, but who cares? You certainly shouldn't. It isn't about you, it's about them and their insecurities. When people say that you need to be "realistic", just keep in mind that to them, being realistic means being negative. No-one who achieves anything does it by thinking small or by setting out thinking it probably isn't going to happen. The right people to be around are those who feel inspired by seeing others living their dream; these are the people who will support you on your journey to achieving yours.

At this point in the discussion, I realised that much of the message I was sending out to Ava revolved around thinking big. She was now, quite rightly, querying how it's possible to think big if you don't know what big is. This is a good point, because what's big for one person might be small for another. To answer her question, I said, "We don't know what we don't know, until we know! Why put a cap on what's possible? Just stay curious, and stay open to and interested in success. Be a lifelong student of life, and make a study of what other big thinkers are doing. Study the habits of successful people. Who is at the top of the field you're interested in? Who is world-renowned in their field, be it nutrition, health and fitness, business, finance, relationships, travel and adventure, philosophy, spirituality, or any other area of a balanced life that is important to you? Identify them, and then apply what you learn about the way they think and their daily habits in your own life."

Making a study of others requires on-going reading and learning. Reading is the foundation of a successful life, but only if you act on what you read. People say that knowledge is power, but this isn't strictly true. Knowledge is potential power. To realise that potential, you need to put it to constructive use. There's no such thing as luck, and nothing happens by chance; everything happens for a reason. Instead of counting on luck, concentrate on developing the qualities that will allow you to become the best you can be.

Ava's next question gave me a little reminder of the difference age can make. She said, "Dad, how do I build a good attitude towards life? I don't always feel confident in myself, and that means I don't always believe I can accomplish what I want. Others in my class always look so confident. How can I become like them?"

Her words took me back to being a teenager myself. It took me years to realise that the people who looked most confident were often faking it. Knowing what I know now, I see that they were right to do it. Perhaps the greatest weakness we humans have is that we sell ourselves short. Life is too short to be little. Something those fakers knew was that if you walk around exuding confidence, even if you're not feeling it, you will come to feel it. It goes both ways: if you walk around exuding fear, convinced that whatever it is, you're not going to be able to do it, then you'll be right – you won't be able to do it.

In response to her question, I said, "No-one is born with confidence. Confidence is acquired and developed. Those people you know in your class who radiate confidence must have acquired their confidence in some way, and so can you. I had to work hard on my confidence, and it's still something I work on. When I feel the need for more confidence, I go to my 'cheat sheet' to remind myself of the steps I need to take, and what works for me. My list might not be your list; therefore, you can develop your own steps or go-to confidence-boosting guide, or whatever you want to call it."

I only know what works for me, but there are 8 rules I follow when I feel my confidence sagging. I'm sure there are many other methods, but here are my confidence boosters:

1. **Act**
   If you don't feel confident, you need to act confident. As the saying goes: fake it till you make it. Always sit in the front row, be conspicuous, and stand out, but for the right reasons. When I lack

confidence, I'm aware of it, so I act confident in the same way an actor would portray a confident character in a film. By acting confident, I soon become confident. Confidence is not something you're born with; it's made. So you can become more confident by *being* confident.

2   **Think Positive**
As James Allen stated in his book *As a Man Thinketh*, it's impossible for positive thoughts and actions not to have positive consequences. The same goes for negative thoughts and actions, in that the consequences they produce can only be negative. It's also impossible to be positive all the time. Unwanted things happen, that's life, but when you feel down for any length of time, you must decide to think positively. Positive thoughts will lead to increased confidence. Right thoughts and right efforts will inevitably bring right results. When I'm low, I read an inspiring book, or listen to a great audiobook or podcast while driving, or listen to uplifting music. Each to their own, but who doesn't feel uplifted after listening to *Eye of the Tiger* by Survivor?

3. **Body Language**
This is closely linked to acting, but your body language, behaviour, and appearance can speak volumes. I remind myself to stand tall and make eye contact with people. I listen attentively when people speak to me, making myself totally present and not distracted by thinking of a response in my mind while the other person is still speaking. It's engaging with people, something that many people in society

really no longer do. There's a shift that has taken place, and instead of engaging in conversation, one person talks at the other for a period of time in a sort of, "I'll let you talk *at* me for a period of time in return for you letting me talk *at* you for the same period of time" exchange. Talking *at* someone is not the same as talking *to* someone, and being talked *at* is different to being talked *to*. If you're actually listening – and hearing, which is by no means the same thing – other people will notice that you're doing it, and they'll be attracted to you. Knowing that people can talk to you will give you confidence. Being an example of good manners and ethical behaviour reflects well on you, and it earns you respect. Being treated with respect also leads to more confidence.

4. **Choose Words Carefully**
   Words are powerful. The words you use and the way you speak say a lot about who you are. Words can build up or tear down, whether they're directed at another or yourself. Words can motivate or discourage, and there are often times when it's best to say nothing at all. Benjamin Franklin once said something wise about remembering not only to say the right thing in the right place but, far more difficult, to leave unsaid the wrong thing at the tempting moment. Choose the words you speak very carefully, because they have the potential to accomplish nearly everything, or destroy almost anything. One negative comment can ruin a person's day. A few might even ruin a person's life. On the flip side, one positive and encouraging comment

can make more difference in an individual's life than you might ever know. The way you speak, your attitude, tone, and choice of words, reflects the person you are and impacts everything around you – including yourself. Choosing your words carefully can greatly contribute to your success, and therefore your confidence.

5. **Focus On Others**
To give rather than to receive will give you the greatest joy. Leave every person that deals with you feeling better about themselves than before. It takes a lot of confidence to be so happy in yourself that there is no need to be self-centred and selfish, always focusing on the other person's needs instead, but know that the universe always balances things out. By focusing on others, the joy you give will be returned to you, and most likely with interest.

6. **Keep Moving**
Walk 25% faster than anyone else, and walk with purpose. You can change your attitude by changing your state or posture through the speed of movement. Use this 25% faster walking technique to help build self-confidence. Straighten your back, lift your head, move ahead just a little faster than anyone else, and you'll see your confidence grow. Choose not to stand to the right with the crowd when going up or down an escalator, be the person who walks past with purpose on the left. I always find it hard to get to the gym, but once I'm there, I know I'm going to walk out a different, more positive, more energised person. Keep moving to keep giving yourself more confidence.

7. **Keep Setting Goals**
Keep setting goals, and know that failure builds confidence. It's a paradox, but failing means you've tried something, and that can never be a bad thing. I've had a go at a few ventures – some I've had success in, others not, but every failure was learning for me. Goals are as essential to success as air is to life. No-one ever stumbles into success without a goal. You will fail along the way, but failing puts you one step closer to reaching your goals, and reaching your goals will build confidence. As Thomas Edison once said, "I have not failed. I've just found 10,000 ways that did not work." Don't be afraid to fail along the way, and never fail to set goals. True failure is our inability to set and reach goals in life. You may not have everything you need when you first turn a dream into a goal, but setting that goal is taking action, and through taking action you begin to attract all you need to succeed into your life.

8. **Dream Big Dreams**
Dream big dreams and believe that they will come true. I've always been a dreamer. A question I ask myself is: if money was of no concern, would I still do what I currently do? Mark 9 says that all things are possible to him who believes. To learn to believe is of primary importance. It's the basic factor of succeeding in any undertaking.

End of Day One

"There's nowhere else like it," is something you'll hear many people say about many places. It's so overused that it isn't usually true, but it *is* true about Iceland. Iceland has always left me spellbound, and the more I wandered from place to place experiencing new countries, it quickly became one of my favourite countries in the world. The locals are warm and welcoming. They are incredibly hospitable, and while locals make any destination better, there is no doubt that it's the magnificence of the natural landscape that does it for me – from geysers to glaciers and waterfalls to landscapes that make you think you're on the moon, not to mention the magical Northern Lights. For me, nothing is more rewarding than a strenuous mountain hike ending in a perfect 39°C natural geothermal pool with a view to die for all to yourself. This is something we'll be experiencing a lot during our trip. If we get really lucky, we will see the Aurora Borealis, and that will be the icing on the cake.

We left the Blue Lagoon around 9pm and drove around 45 minutes back to our Airbnb in Reykjavik. The drive back was a quiet one. I was quietly pleased at the way Day One had turned out, and I was hoping that Ava's silence meant that she was meditating on some of the points we'd discussed. It was the slight snoring noise coming from my right that made that hope crumble. *Ah, well*, I thought, *let the start not define the end. Tomorrow is another day.*

Chapter 3
Your Journey to Happiness

"When I was 5 years old, my mother always told me that happiness was the key to life. When I went to school, they asked me what I wanted to be when I grew up. I wrote down 'happy'. They told me I didn't understand the assignment, and I told them they didn't understand life." – John Lennon

Day 2: Reykjavik to Vik

We get up early in order to hit the road and make the most of the few hours of daylight we would have. Today we are driving from Reykjavik to Vik, with a few stops along the way. We pack our bags into the car, with coffee ready for the road. This is going to be an ambitious travel day for us. The Golden Circle consists of Pingviller National Park, the geysers at Haukadalur, and the Gullfoss waterfall, making it one of the most popular tourist routes in Iceland.

It will take just under two hours to reach our first stop at Seljalandsfoss waterfall. Falling 213 feet over an old sea cliff, Seljalandsfoss is one of the most well-known waterfalls in Iceland. If you don't mind getting wet, you can even walk all the way behind the falls for a unique view. There's a restroom there, a small shop, and a stand that serves sandwiches and cake if you need a snack. From there, we'll go to the nearby Skogafoss waterfall. This will be quite an action-packed part of the day because we'll go next to see the geysers and the Eyjafjallajokull Volcano Visitor Centre, which is about 15 minutes from Seljalandsfoss, and the warm interior will make it difficult to leave again on a rainy, cold day like today. There, we'll watch a video about the 2010 volcanic eruption.

People all over the world remember that eruption because it cancelled huge numbers of flights between places a long way away (I remember someone telling me that their flight from Dubai to Manchester had been cancelled), but this video is about its impact on the local people. When you live somewhere like the UK, you don't expect to experience an erupting volcano during your lifetime, but it's something the Icelanders have to live with. As the name is the letter E followed by 15 more letters, the centre is usually referred to as E-15. Ava made it clear that she was more than happy to go along with that abbreviation.

When we've seen everything we want to see at E-15, we'll drive to Reynisfjara Beach. The beach is about 10 minutes from Vik, and what makes it unmissable is the black sand and the basalt columns of Reynisfjall mountain, which resemble something you might expect to find on a far distant planet. These rock formations are completely natural, and the massive basalt cave has been continuously carved and shaped by the sea. Reynisfjara Beach is said to be an eerie experience on rainy, foggy days like today, so we should be in for a treat there, and then we'll head to Vik, where we'll spend the night.

"Well, that all sounds very exciting," said Ava, as I finished describing the day ahead. "Let's hit the road!" And so, we did.

Hitting the Road to Vik

Driving east from Reykjavik, across landscape that makes you think you're driving on Mars; we see the first rays of sun trying to fight through the fog and rain. Sipping on a warm coffee, I ask Ava whether she's given any more thought to what she wants to do after school. Although she's talked recently about medical school, there was a time when she wanted to be a pilot or an architect – she'd been very creative when she was younger, always building all sorts of things. As a father, I find this a pressing topic, but Ava is 14 and probably feels that she still has lots of time to decide. By rights she should have, but that isn't the way the system works; just three years from now she's going to be applying to university, and the courses open to her will have a great deal to do with the decisions she makes now. Is it fair to place that kind of burden on a 14-year-old? No, it probably isn't, but it's how things are, and we have to deal with it.

Ava says, "After school, I want to start by travelling a bit. You and Mum have certainly given me a passion for travel, and I'm hoping that I'll gain a better idea of what I want to do by the time I come back. The only thing I know for certain is that I want to always stay happy."

Well, there was some interesting stuff in that answer, and above all, that Ava wanted to stay happy. This meant she must consider herself happy now, so at least her mother and I could think we'd had some success in raising her, because being happy as a teenager can be challenging. I remember having many internal struggles myself in my teens.

"What do you think will make you happy in the future?" I asked.

"Not too sure, Dad," came the reply. "What made you happy when you were my age?"

What is Happiness?

What indeed? And is it relevant? Each of us is unique. What made and still makes me happy might not make someone else happy, and we change as we grow older. When I was Ava's age, being with my friends made me happy. Sunday barbeques, or braais as we call them back home, with the family made me happy. Watching movies made me happy. Many things made me happy in my teens, especially growing up in a happy home, but evidence suggests that some things are more consistently associated with happiness. Studies suggest that genuine happiness is linked to being happy with who you are and what you have, being humble and not envying what others have, having great relationships with people and leading a healthy lifestyle. Happiness, therefore, is being you as your best self, so look no further than yourself to find it.

An acquaintance of mine has been through some tough times recently. He had some symptoms he didn't care for, and the doctors said he was suffering from long Covid. He says, "I accepted that at first, but after a CT scan, an ECG, two echocardiograms, an ultrasound, and more blood tests than you can shake a stick at, I realised that long Covid was just the easy diagnosis. The fact is, they don't know what's the matter with me, and neither do I. They don't know whether I'm going to get better, stay the same, or go downhill – and neither do I. I have my bad days, believe me, I do, but I'm still here. You know that song by Stephen Sondheim, *I'm Still Here*? It's sung by someone who's been through everything the 20th century could throw at them and survived. That's how I feel. I'm still here, and you want to know the funny thing, I'm still happy."

I thought this was a fairly remarkable thing – that someone who didn't know whether he was going to live or die could still describe himself as happy. When I asked what made him happy, he said, "It's simple. All right, I've always been an optimist, a glass half full person, but why am I happy? Because I'm doing what I want to do, I live in a place that's where I want to be, and I do the job I always wanted to do – writing. And people pay me for it, not a fortune, but you don't need a fortune to be rich in the things that matter. There are lots of things I can't have because I can't afford them, but I don't want any of them, so who cares? There isn't anything I really want that I can't have.

"There was a time in my life when I wasn't a writer. I was Sales Director of a fairly large IT company, I made the kind of money most people can only dream about, and I hated it. I hated the job, hated the person I was turning into, hated the conversations I had with people who worked with me, so I gave it up because it was killing me. I sold my great big status symbol of a house and moved to somewhere I could buy for cash. It's way out in the sticks, where I have more four-legged than two-legged neighbours, I'm working at what I want to work at, and I'm here. I'm alive. Who needs more than that?"

The last bit really resonated with me because I believe that's the way people feel when they are happy – they feel alive. But I also believe that we need to be realistic in that life won't always be happy, that's just the way it is, and we are going to experience problems along the way. Ava knows it's possible to cope with problems and come through stronger on the other side, something she says she has learned from her mother and me, so that's good. But we were about to go down another rabbit hole when I said, "I believe your life must have meaning if you want to be truly happy." In response to this, Ava wanted to know what I meant by "meaning".

The Meaning of Meaning

I believe that a person really lives if they experience life as having meaning and value, and if they have something to live for. As soon as meaning, value, and hope vanish from a person's experience, that person begins to stop living and starts to just exist.

Tony Robbins once said that if you don't grow, you die. This might sound overly dramatic, but it simply makes the point that life is for living, not just merely existing.

To my mind, we need to keep growing and always keep searching for our own meaning in life, even in our old age. Looking at it this way helps to explain why there are many wealthy people in the world who still feel unsatisfied in life. It's also why a lot of older people know from their own experience that a long life without a feeling of accomplishment or of being needed is wearisome.

"So, Dad, you're saying that being wealthy and growing to an old age will not bring you happiness?" questioned Ava.

Was I saying that? No, I wasn't. We need money to survive, and we need a certain level of income to thrive, but being wealthy and living to a great age are not in themselves enough. To answer her question, I said, "I believe that God wants us to thrive. Take my writer friend as an example. When he was young, he thought he would have happiness when he had become what the world believes is successful and wealthy. Then, when he had those things, he realised that happiness was further away than it had been when he was at school and his greatest ambition was to be opening batsman in the first eleven. Was it success that made him happy, or does happiness have to come before success? It's counterintuitive, but I think it's the latter."

While we were on the topic, something else I wanted to pass on to Ava is that happiness is contagious. If you surround yourself with genuinely happy people, it will rub off on you, and if you're happy, your happiness will rub off on other people. If you focus on being happy in yourself, the people you meet will feel that happiness and will want to be around you. There's a need for self-awareness. If your mood is low, you need to acknowledge it and ask yourself why, and then take action to lift yourself into a better mood. When you wake up each morning at the beginning of a new day, you're going to be in a good mood or a bad mood. Something I think a lot of people struggle to understand is that you can choose. So, choose. When you wake up each day, decide to be in a good mood.

My advice to Ava at this point was, "Don't take yourself too seriously. Laugh at yourself because I believe that laughter is the great secret of living life. If you bring laughter into your life, you'll live longer, so make it a habit to be happy." The point I was making is that it's important not to postpone your happiness by saying you'll be happy when you have this, or you'll be happy when you achieve that – that's not how happiness works. I said, "Decide to be happy now, right here in the car. Let's both decide that today is going to be a happy day."

Perhaps one way of thinking about this is to think of it as baking a cake. Just as you have a recipe for baking a cake, there's a recipe for happiness. It's going to be an individual thing, but for me, the main ingredients in the recipe for true happiness are:

- contentment and generosity
- being of sound health and mind
- having love as your strongest ally
- forgiving freely (and by that, I mean forgiving yourself as well as others)

- continuously learning through having positive goals, dreams, and aspirations that push you outside your comfort zone
- and ultimately loving and serving God.

Contentment and Generosity

"Ava, how often have you heard that happiness and success are measured in terms of assets or wealth?"

"Never," said Ava. "No-one ever says that, but you can tell by the way they behave it's what they think."

What Ava was saying is true. Millions work long, exhausting hours to make more money, but I was hoping that our conversation was helping to ensure she didn't fall into the trap of thinking money and possessions bring lasting happiness. They don't. Experience tells us that once our basic needs are met, more income does little to improve our overall happiness or our sense of well-being. Money itself is not the issue. I see money as a protection. We need money to survive and a bit more to thrive, but continuously striving for more money is linked to unhappiness, not happiness, and it's a growing concern in society.

I asked Ava if she had heard of the 996-work culture. In China, this culture has become the way to live. People work from nine in the morning till nine at night, six days a week, and it's a work habit that's at the heart of the Chinese people's climb from poverty to prosperity. Of course, the question is: does it make them happy? I don't believe it does, and even the Chinese government has come to the realisation that all is not well. They're trying to get companies to wean themselves off the 996 culture, but they're not going to find it easy. I've been through this myself. I'd lie awake for hours at night, worrying about money and anxious for the future. Then, when I'd made the money to buy whatever shiny thing I thought I needed, I'd lie awake again for hours wondering why the promised happiness had not arrived with it. I worried when investments failed, and I was well and truly caught up in the drive to always have more, to have bigger, to have better.

The problem here is that the craving for more money can never be satisfied. The Bible says that a lover of silver will never be satisfied with silver, nor a lover of wealth with income. Solomon learned that a life of self-indulgence ultimately leaves one feeling empty and unfulfilled, but that's not saying there's anything wrong with money. Ava was clearly relieved to learn this, saying, "I thought you were going to tell me I had to live without it."

This made me smile. "I'd like to see you try. You'd have to find a desert island, cut yourself off entirely from the world, and live on coconuts. We need to remember that the Bible doesn't have anything bad to say about money. What it says is that the *love* of money is the root of all evil. The love of money, not money itself. You have to be content with what you have, but that doesn't mean giving up ambition and settling for a mediocre life. Far from it. What we all have to do is focus on the things we enjoy doing and want to do. The money we want – the money that does us good instead of damaging our lives – is the money that comes from following our passions and dreams."

I thought about what I'd just said, and I couldn't see any holes in it. But I'd missed something. There's something that goes along with an unhealthy love of money for its own sake, and that's envy. It should be a case of you have what you have, I have what I have, and other people have what they have, but all too often we see people wasting their time envying what other people have. They envy others instead of concentrating on their own dreams and generating more of what they want for themselves. Envy is an illness. If you let it, it can take over your life and destroy your happiness.

Ava thought about this, then asked, "But, Dad, can we not be inspired by people who have what we want, and learn from them?"

"Of course, we can," was my answer. "In fact, you should. You should try hard to associate yourself with people who inspire you in ways that can help you to grow, but that's ambition, not envy." I explained my thoughts on this by returning to the success of Emma Raducanu. Ambition is being inspired to do better by the example of someone else. A Grand Slam winner at 18, Emma's success has inspired others to focus on what they want to achieve for themselves. It has shown others what can be achieved when you *plan* and *prepare* to succeed, and you're prepared to put plans into action. Ambition is healthy, envy is not. If you're simply envying the girl in school whose parents have more money than your parents and always seems to have the latest fashions, the latest smartphone, and holidays in whatever exotic place is deemed the "in" place to be seen, that's envy. Envy won't inspire you to *do* anything, or focus your thoughts on planning how to achieve the things you want for yourself in life.

At this point, Ava questioned how she would know when she was being inspired by someone and when she was just feeling envious. This was a question I could answer simply and quickly: 'If you see a friend succeeding at something, do you feel delighted for the friend, or do you feel deflated because they have something you don't have?'

Ava understood this right away – delighted equals inspired; deflated equals envious. Another way to think about it is to consider how you respond when a friend fails at something. Do you feel sad on the friend's behalf and try to make them feel better, or are you secretly glad they failed? Being glad in that situation is pure envy. Envy can poison a person's capacity to enjoy the good things in life, and reduce the feelings of gratitude for life's many gifts. I don't think anyone will ever have found happiness like that, nor health for that matter.

Your Health Is Your Wealth

The link between happiness and health is direct and inescapable. Your health will be your wealth, especially as you grow older. Most things we do affect our health, our mindset, and our overall wellbeing. If you ever want a reminder that life is simply not fair, just take a look at how people vary in the matter of health. There are some who live in a way that seems to ignore all doctors' advice, and yet they scarcely know a day's illness. When they celebrate their 100th birthday and a journalist ask them for the secret of long life, they put it down to a cigar and a large Scotch every evening (and that's just the women). Others adhere to every recommendation put forward by the medical profession, and yet still suffer the kind of chronic ill health that has a major impact on their life.

I remember how the diagnosis of Type 1 diabetes changed my life. Within a day, I went from taking life for granted to being in hospital with drips in my arms and doctors telling me that from now on I'd need to inject myself four times a day with insulin. If I don't – if I neglect things as I did in the past – I will die. Imminent death certainly changes one's perspective. Paradox it may be, but I always say I believe T1D saved my life. When you realise how quickly life can change, you look at life differently. I focused more on my personal development, my relationships, my spirituality, and my health. I realised that if I wanted to see Ava grow old and see my grandchildren, I had to act, and live a healthier, more balanced life. I had to do some serious introspection and be honest with myself. I needed to identify all my bad habits and the consequences of bad choices made in the past. No-one really knows what brings on T1D, but there is a school of thought that says it's related to long periods of high stress and an unhealthy overall lifestyle. What it means is that your overall wellbeing, and therefore your happiness, is directly related to your health.

"Am I doing enough?" Ava wanted to know. "I'm active in school sport, I get enough sleep, and I eat what Mum makes us. What more can I do?"

I was able to assure her that everything she was doing was good. It's believed that sleep, sunshine, diet, and exercise create the foundation for good health. Having an Italian mother who loves to cook great food doesn't make eating in moderation easy. What she likes to cook, we like to eat, and my waistline confirms that. It's fair to say that living in England does limit the amount of sunshine we're likely to see, but overall, Ava has a healthy lifestyle. I then added, "There are other elements that can help towards a healthier life. One of them is not polluting your body with anything harmful.

"That 100-year-old woman who said she got there on a daily cigar and a glass of whisky is an exception rather than a norm. It may have worked for her, but for most people, smoking leads to disease and disability and harms nearly every organ in your body. I agree with people who say you need to experiment in life and stay curious, but messing with things where the likely outcome is already known is not experimenting. We all develop habits, often without knowing it, and a good question to ask yourself is: what do you do when no-one is watching you? That's when you are really you, so what are you doing during your free time?" I made it clear I wasn't expecting Ava to give me an answer to that question, but I did suggest it might be something she could consider answering for herself.

It seems to me that it's important to understand that life is not an accident. It's a gift, and we shouldn't take it for granted. Appreciating life as a gift will move you to avoid taking needless risks. A momentary thrill is not worth a life of disability. You also need to control your negative emotions. Your mind and body are closely linked. Try to avoid undue anxiety, anger, and envy. Instead, focus on positive thoughts. Your thoughts drive your actions. If you think negatively, you will feel negative. People have talked for years about the power of positive thinking, and the reason for this is that it works. You *can* manifest what you constantly think about. No good can ever come from a negative mindset, so trying to maintain a positive outlook, even when you're experiencing problems, is the only way to get through those difficulties. In the same way that children are told not to pull horrible faces because one day the wind will change and their face will be stuck like that, constantly thinking negative thoughts can lead to getting stuck in negative thinking, and then negative, envious, hate-filled thoughts will come to define you. You won't be happy.

Victim culture seems to perpetuate negativity. It's almost as if people want to be seen as a victim of something, and if you take a hard look at those people, you see they never have a moment of happiness. I've never once thought of my T1D in a negative way, or as a disability. I've never thought, *why me?* I refuse to be a victim. Me, a victim? How can I be a victim when the way I think, the way I act, and my mental wellbeing have all improved in so many ways? There's a corny old saying: "If life hands you lemons, make lemonade." It's corny, but it's the way to be. If you've taken a blow that has knocked you flat, it's unfortunate and it may well leave you feeling discouraged for a while, but it can only be for a while. You need to bounce back; you need to adapt and find ways to cope. This can sound easier said than done, but it's the *doing* that will make you feel better. Adapting, coping, and finding a way will make you feel good about yourself. You'll be happy. Mission accomplished.

Love Yourself, Love Others, Love God

Love, for me, is perhaps the most important ingredient in the recipe for happiness. Always cultivate love in your life. Love yourself, love others, love God. Love is by far our most powerful emotion, and love sometimes make us do crazy things. In saying this to Ava, she instantly wanted to know what those "crazy things" were. I thought about things like driving for 12 hours just to see someone for an hour before they fly out somewhere, or standing in the rain at midnight crying when you see your "girlfriend's" car parked in front of another boy's house… and then I thought that these things are perhaps a conversation for another day when Ava is older.

Instead, I answered her question by saying that love can make you do crazy things, probably bordering on being creepy, but love is also what turns work into a passion rather than a job. Love turns a couple into a family. Love turns a house into a home. Love surely is the most powerful emotion we have, which is probably why we crave it. No marriage, no family, no friendship can thrive without it, and nor can happiness, mental health, or overall wellbeing.

One of the problems that arises when talking about love is that it has more often than not come to mean romantic love, or even carnal love. While the first of those is of course important – choosing the wrong partner is a quick shortcut to unhappiness – the love I'm talking about is the kind that causes a person to show sincere concern for the welfare of others, even putting them before self. It is love guided by godly principles, but it isn't by any means lacking in warmth and feeling. There's a verse in the Bible that describes it very well. It says: "Love is patient and kind. Love is not jealous. It does not brag, does not get puffed up, does not behave indecently, does not look for its own interests, does not become provoked. It does not keep account of injury. It does not rejoice over unrighteousness but rejoices in the truth. It bears all things, hopes all things, endures all things. Love never fails."

Isn't that beautiful? It may be from the Bible, but you don't need to be religious to experience it. It never fails. It will never cease to exist. In fact, it can grow stronger over time, and because it is patient, kind, and forgiving, it is a perfect bond. You can have two very imperfect individuals, but they can still be bound by that love and, if they are, they will feel both secure and happy. The sheer importance of love is that people's feelings about their relationships have a bigger impact on their overall satisfaction with their lives than do their careers, their income, their community, or even their physical health. To be genuinely happy for other people's success and sad when they fail, that is the love I believe to be the foundation for all happiness.

However, it's important not to ignore self-love. Shakespeare said it nicely in Henry V: "Self-love, my liege, is not so vile a sin as self-neglecting." How right he was. The key to helping others, and therefore being happy, is to love yourself first. The best contribution you can make in terms of helping someone else in life is to keep working on your own personal development. If you become 10 times wiser and 10 times stronger, think of the improvement this represents in your ability to help others and build stronger relationships. James Allen said that the secret of abounding happiness is to forget yourself in all that you do and lose yourself in the welfare of others. It's good advice, although there's just one thing I'd like to add: make sure that it really is the welfare of others that's your concern. It may be a little too easy to simply be nosy.

Forgive Freely

Holding grudges against people doesn't hurt them; it only hurts you. If you want to be happy, forgive freely. As Ava quickly pointed out, this isn't always so easy, but let's face it, lots of worthwhile things aren't easy. It may be difficult, but forgiveness is important, whether it's forgiving others or yourself. One of the hardest things we have to do as human beings is to recognise when we're in the wrong. If we've done something we shouldn't have done, perhaps causing hurt to others or perhaps just letting ourselves down, we need to find the maturity to own it. Maturity is being able to accept what you did, accept that it was wrong, say sorry for having done it, and mean it when you say you won't do it again, and then forgive yourself so that you can move on. If you don't mean what you say, you're not ready to move on.

Ava wondered why it was so important to go through this process of forgiveness, so I put it this way: "When someone does something wrong to you – or when you think someone has, which comes to the same thing in your head – you're likely to be filled with anger, resentment, or even thoughts of revenge. Those thoughts and feelings are damaging, not to the other person, but to you. When you forgive, you let go of all those bad things. It's a popular belief that John Wayne once said, 'Forgive your enemy – but remember the bastard's name.' If he did, or if anyone did, that isn't forgiveness. The harm you're doing to yourself won't go away if you think like that. You have to forgive properly. This doesn't mean having to condone what someone did when it was wrong, and it doesn't mean minimising it or pretending it didn't happen. Forgiveness isn't any of those things, it's a well thought out personal choice that reflects a loving commitment to peace and to building or maintaining a good relationship with the other person.

No-one is perfect, and when you forgive, you show that you know that. A forgiving person understands that we all stumble sometimes and say and do things that we're sorry for. Quite often, we feel regret the moment we say or do whatever it was we shouldn't have said or done." To help Ava understand this, I told her that I couldn't count the number of heated conversations I'd had with my mother – her grandmother – and then put the phone down, only to immediately phone back to apologise. "Never be too proud to apologise," I said, adding, "I also remember not speaking to your uncle for almost a year over something silly. Sometimes your ego can be your worst enemy. That year of not speaking to your uncle was not a very happy period in my life. Being so unforgiving, angry, and bitter over something silly obviously soured our relationship, and I'm not too proud to admit that it led to loneliness as your uncle was the only family I had in England. Sometimes people can become so focused on a wrong that they can't get on with enjoying life."

Being so easily offended can lead to increased stress levels and a higher risk of depression and other health problems. Life is too short. Say you're sorry, fix the breach, and move on in peace. When I take a moment to think about the unhappiest people I've known, they have had all kinds of different characteristics, but one thing they have all had in common is a grievance, and it's never a grievance they're looking to overcome, offset, or forget. They nurture it. I've learned that if you freely forgive those who offend you and ask for forgiveness from those you offend, you will have healthier relationships, your mental and spiritual well-being will improve, and you'll have less anxiety and stress.

I said to Ava, "Forgiving yourself, by the way, becomes a lot easier if you accept that you're not perfect. You make mistakes. Don't cover them up – learn from them. And be patient with yourself. You won't get rid of every personality flaw and bad habit overnight. Associate with friends who are encouraging, positive, and kind, but who will also be honest with you. If you hurt someone, take responsibility for it and be quick to apologise. When you make peace, you gain inner peace and resilience. You must recognise that mistakes and failure are a natural occurrence, but how you respond to these events is up to you. When people who are resilient make mistakes, they don't berate themselves with self-defeating language such as 'I'm a failure' or 'I'm useless', they accept what is, learn, and then they forget about it to concentrate on their goals."

Have Big Scary Goals

Why is it so important to have goals? A goal is something you want to achieve in the future. It can be short-term or very long-term, and in fact, most of us need a combination of short-term, medium-term, and long-term goals. A goal shouldn't be something that's going to happen anyway, so leaving school, for example, is not a goal. Leaving school with three A-star A-levels would be a goal, but it's not necessarily a goal for everyone. What defines a goal is that it involves planning, flexibility, and action. If all of those things are present then, whatever it is, you have a goal.

To answer the question of why goals are important, it's because reaching them can boost your confidence, strengthen your friendships, and increase your happiness. When you set small goals and reach them, you gain the confidence to take on bigger ones. Little victories also lead to a feeling of greater self-worth, and you feel more confident when facing day-to-day challenges – such as standing up to peer pressure. It's also fair to say that people enjoy being around those who are goal-oriented, meaning those who know what they want and are willing to work for it. Moreover, one of the best ways to strengthen a friendship is to work with another person toward a common goal.

Goals keep you focused. They give you something to keep reaching for, and when you set and reach goals, you feel a sense of accomplishment. Achieving a goal feels great, allowing you to look back over your journey and say, "Wow, I really did it! I accomplished what I set out to do." For me, the goal of going to the gym can be a challenge, but by aiming for something such as running a marathon or taking part in a cycling event in four months' time, going to the gym is no longer the goal in itself; it's just part of the journey to reaching the outcome I want.

Something I've discovered to be true is that you get the results you expect. It's often said, but it has been my own experience that if you expect mediocre results, those are the results you get. This may not come as a surprise to anyone, but it's a little more surprising when you consider that if you expect big results, you get big results. I found this to be true by pushing myself. I kept setting myself bigger goals, and then even bigger goals, and bigger still, until I was setting myself big scary goals. These goals weren't so big and scary that I'd never be able to achieve them – for example, challenging myself to run a marathon in under two hours would have been counterproductive – they were goals that I could build on to keep progressing. (Perhaps aiming to beat my previous marathon time in the next marathon).

Ava's interest was piqued by this, and she asked, "What steps do you think I can take to reach my goals?"

"Well, for me, rule number one is to get your mindset right," was my reply. "The first thing is to accept that you are where you are today based on past decisions and actions. This is something that's very important to understand. Think of a guy just coming to the end of a prison sentence. As I see it, there are two routes someone in that position might normally take. One is to come to terms with what got them into the mess in the first place, the other is to blame other people, or circumstances, or both. By taking the first choice, they're saying, 'It was my fault. No-one made me do it. I did something I shouldn't have done, and I paid the penalty,' and in so doing, they're putting themselves in a position to move forward. By taking the other choice, they're saying, 'It wasn't my fault. I was stabbed in the back/let down/misinformed,' or, 'the police set me up,' or, 'the sentence I got was far too harsh for what I did,' and in so doing, they're very likely to find themselves in trouble again. Why? Well, if it wasn't his fault, why should he change?"

"Dad! I'm not planning to do anything that will land me in jail!"

"I'm glad to hear it, and I'm sure you won't end up there, but this applies to everything we do. You see, whatever position we find ourselves in, we got there because of what we did or what we didn't do."

This prompted Ava to question whether some people just have advantages in life that others don't have. It's certainly true in that some people are born to parents with far more money than other people's parents. They go to immensely expensive schools, and the education they get puts them way ahead of anyone else competing for the same job. As if that's not enough of an advantage, they have a network of well-connected people they met at school, and influential people they know through their parents. These people are probably going to remain richer than others throughout their lives, but the message here is so important that I wanted her to imagine I'd written it on a huge banner that was being dragged behind an airplane for all to read:

It isn't the hand you're dealt that counts. It's how you play the cards.

You have to take responsibility for yourself, meaning responsibility for what you've done and for what you haven't done. Don't blame other people if you don't reach your goals; there's only one person responsible for your destiny, and that person is you. Ava thought this sounded a little harsh, so I told her the story of Jimmy Greaves.

Coming from South Africa, football isn't really my game, but when ex-player Jimmy Greaves died, it was hard to miss the outpouring of grief that seemed to come from all angles around England. In the obituaries, it was said that Jimmy Greaves was the only natural born goal scorer England has ever produced. With this being the case, he can't really claim credit for his skills, but the fact remains that they gave him a great career for which he is still remembered by football fans all over England. Whatever club people support, and however much hostility they may feel towards the clubs Greaves played for, they suspend that hostility when it comes to him. When his playing days were over, little by little and bit by bit he started to drink too much. He became an alcoholic and brought his life to ruins.

There was no-one to blame but himself. His skills may have been a natural gift, but nature couldn't be blamed for his drinking. However, he realised this and recognised what he had done to himself and to the family he loved. He got himself off the bottle, got back together with his wife, and built a whole new career for himself on television with another ex-footballer. The key to his redemption was his willingness to take responsibility. He accepted responsibility for the mess he'd made – he got himself into it, and he got himself out of it. Greaves wasn't born with the silver spoon of advantage in his mouth, his father was a guard on a bus, but he made maximum use of the gift nature had given him. Crucially, he also knew when it was time to say, "I've been in the wrong, I'm responsible, and I'm going to change." He took the hand he'd been dealt, and he played the cards to maximum effect, and this makes him someone we can all admire.

The message I wanted Ava to receive is that the mindset Jimmy Greaves adopted is the mindset you need to succeed in life. You need to truly believe you can reach your goals; that you have what it takes – the talent, will, drive, and time to reach your goals. Having a positive mindset and a clear vision of what you want to achieve is very important, but you also need to have an abundance mindset. This is often the hardest thing to achieve, as people tend to think of everything as a competition. There's a belief that for you to achieve your goals, others will need to miss theirs, and this simply isn't true. An abundance mindset is the belief that there's plenty going around for everyone to win. All it takes is the belief that the universe has enough for everyone. Set yourself a goal, reach it, and then look around and see that you haven't prevented others from reaching theirs. Do that often enough, and you'll be convinced that there *is* enough for everyone. When you've got that firmly in your mind, you not only have a positive mindset, but you also have an abundance mindset – you've reached ground zero.

At this point, Ava was clearly beginning to think about things. She said, "This is sounding like a huge challenge. It sounds like I do all the work to get my head straight and set my goals, and then after that I'm still just at the beginning?"

In response, I agreed that it *is* a huge challenge, but also made the point that it should be. When it's your life and how you're going to live it that you're talking about, you can't expect it to be easy. However, it's not an impossible challenge. Once your mindset is focused on your goal, you need to make your plan and look at the actions or steps you'll need to take to get there. This is going to be a case of different strokes for different folks, but what works for me is to start by identifying my goals in writing. For this purpose, I have a journal in which I can write down the goals I want to achieve. It has been said by some wise people that in writing down your goals, you're already halfway there. So, I always start by writing them down. Once I have my list, I prioritise them. I usually choose the biggest goal as my top priority and, funnily enough, the biggest goal is often the scariest goal, but I'm a firm believer in tackling my scariest goals first.

Once I have my list in priority order, I start planning. I need to set realistic deadlines; I need to break the end goal down into smaller steps or goals; and I also need to anticipate obstacles and think about how to overcome them. But, most importantly, I need to take action. A goal without action is just a dream. It's said that knowledge is power, but knowledge doesn't become power until it's applied. Don't wait until you have every detail worked out to get started. Ask yourself, "What is the very first thing I can do toward reaching my goal?" Then do it. Lastly, I track my progress as I complete each step. Some people also believe in telling other people their goals, on the basis that you won't want to lose face by saying you're going to do something and then not doing it. Personally, I prefer not telling anyone and just letting my actions talk for themselves. This is something everyone needs to work out for themselves, but it's not a process that's gone through once and then forgotten about; it's something that will go on throughout your life.

It didn't take Ava long to raise a flaw she'd seen in my argument. "Dad, you said we all need to show gratitude and be content with what we have, but now you say I have to set goals for the rest of my life. How does that work?"

My answer to this was that lasting happiness doesn't come from what we've done or what we have. Like good physical health, it doesn't just happen; it's a process. Once you've reached a health level that you and your doctor are happy with, it needs to be maintained or there's potential to become unhealthy again. It's the same with setting goals and growing as a person. It's a lifelong cycle of starting and completing goals, and many of them will need to be maintained after they're achieved. It sounds like hard work, but it's worth it.

The type of goals you set will contribute to the happiness they bring. Not all goals produce the same benefits, and some can be downright bad for you and your eventual happiness. Imagine setting yourself the goal of climbing the corporate ladder as fast as you can and creating a plan that's based on doing whatever it takes to get there. You wouldn't be alone with this goal, and on the surface, it may seem positive, inspirational, and ambitious, but there can be a whole host of problems that arise from the way you're setting out to achieve it. The steps that some choose to take to achieve this goal can have detrimental effects on others, and not infrequently, they're also detrimental to themselves. For example, you might give up valuable family time to reach this goal, or you might give up focusing on your health. You might even abandon the values you were raised to live by – how many people do you know who got all the way to the top of the tree, and how many of them cheated, lied, and used other people to get there? I sometimes think it might be more productive to ask how many didn't do those things.

Your Values

Values are the personal standards you choose to live by. For example, striving to be honest in everything you do. Our values reflect what's important to us in life, and while we may have a variety of shorter-term goals that are specific to a situation, our values are life goals, and they don't change to meet different situations. Values guide our behaviour in all aspects of our life, including our home life, our work life, and our social life.

I once talked to a guy who had spent 40 years in international sales. He commented that you don't spend that amount of time in Africa, the Middle East, and Asia without seeing a lot of corruption and a great deal of bribery. Something he said that I found very interesting was, "Other people are taking bribes. You don't see the bribe itself, because those transactions are hidden. People are ashamed of them, so they do them in secret. But you know the bribe has been paid; you can tell by the changed behaviour in the person who took the bribe, and what you need to remember is that sooner or later, the bribe is going to be offered to *you*. That's when you find out what your values really are. If you're tempted, just remember that someone will know you took the bribe – someone always knows, and they'll adjust their view of you accordingly." Are you up for that? Are you ready to have people looking down on you, disrespecting you, regarding you as someone of little value because of something you did?

That, to me, says everything you need to know about values. Your values are what you will be judged by. Sticking to good values, or not, is always your choice.

End of Day Two

We arrived in Vik around three in the afternoon and it was already pitch dark. Vik is the largest town in the east of Iceland, with a bustling population of about 300 people. Sitting right on the Ring Road, it's the most southern town in the country. In the summer, this means it's a place that stays light for a very long time, with places further north staying light even longer. However, at this time of year, the sun was already long gone for the day – although further north, it would have been gone even earlier.

Shetland is the northernmost part of Britain, and it has the same pattern – in the height of summer it pretty well never gets dark, and in the depths of winter you could never really describe it as light, even in the middle of the day. Shetland's latitude is 60°9'16.42"N. Vik's latitude is 61° 03' 25.63" N. That's less than a full degree north of Shetland. But, once you reach Shetland, you can't go any further north without leaving Britain. Vik is Iceland's southern tip. Head north in winter and there'll be even less light and even more dark.

Despite its small size, Vik is the largest settlement for some 70km around, making it an important staging post that's indicated on road signs from a long distance away. It's an important service centre for the inhabitants of and visitors to the coastal strip between Skógar and the west edge of the Mýrdalssandur glacial outwash plain. It lies directly south of the Mýrdalsjökull glacier, which itself is on top of the Katla Volcano. Katla has not erupted since 1918 and, as this is longer than a typical dormant period, there has been speculation that an eruption may occur soon. I'm just hoping it won't be during our stay.

We stayed at the Volcano Hotel and were welcomed by the friendly and helpful staff. They recommended the Halldorskaffi restaurant for dinner, and we enjoyed some Icelandic pizza and burgers. Another awesome day in this fantastic country.

Chapter 4
Build Powerful Habits

"Depending on what they are, our habits will either make us or break us. We become what we repeatedly do." – Sean Covey

Day 3: Skaftafell and Jokulsarlon

You don't always get what you want, and as it turned out, these words were more than just a line from a Mick Jagger song. We had wanted to begin the third day of our holiday on the black sand beach, but the rain was torrential, and it didn't look like the sort of weather that might improve soon. We'd always known that itineraries have to be changeable at this time of year in Iceland, so we chose to move on to the Skaftafell National Park.

Our drive there was punctuated with a couple of stops at interesting locations that caught our attention. One was Laki lava fields. You drive through miles and miles of lava fields covered in moss, and while you might think there's nothing interesting or beautiful about moss, a visit to the Laki lava fields might just change your mind. On arrival at Skaftafell, we asked the staff in the visitor centre how challenging the hike to the Svartifoss waterfall was. We were informed that it was a nice easy hike and should take about 40 minutes. Well, in my opinion, they lied! It wasn't easy at all, as the entire walk is uphill, and then the final section as you approach the waterfall involves a slippery downhill slope through snow and mud that I found a tad scary.

However, I'm not the bravest when it comes to hiking, so perhaps others would go along with the description of this route being an easy hike.

Despite the challenges involved, walking is a good time for conversation. Ava was interested in knowing more about nurturing good habits. I'd said it was something we all needed to do, but this was now prompting her to ask how. I began by explaining that to be able to nurture good habits and kick bad habits, you first of all need to recognise the habits you have. This can be a problem, as habits are generally things you've come to do without consciously being aware of doing them. If you think about it, it's often other people that point out habits – annoying or otherwise – that you have, and you'll very often not have noticed any of these behaviours yourself. We are all creatures of habit, we all have good and bad habits, so we can all promote better habits and rid ourselves of bad habits once we're aware of them. But it's a process, and it begins with the words you use.

Words Are Powerful

I have a great respect for words; after all, this whole book depends on them. Words have power. The Book of Proverbs says: *"Thoughtless speech is like the stabs of a sword, but the tongue of the wise is a healing."* Sometimes, wisdom lies in knowing when to keep quiet, and when you do speak, you should always try to use words and language that uplifts and encourages. This not only applies to the words you use when speaking to others, but also to yourself. Use words that transcend love, and they'll set you apart. Use big, powerful, positive, and cheerful words and phrases. To help Ava understand what I meant by this, I said, "If someone asks how you are, don't respond by saying that you're tired. Don't invite the person to ask you again at the end of the day. Say that you're fine, even when you're not, and then ask the other person how he or she is. Or, if you find yourself having to describe someone else, use bright, cheerful, favourable words. If you can't, don't say anything about them. There are going to be times when you're upset and you might want to use negative language regarding the person who upset you. It's a natural inclination, but it needs to be avoided. Positive language encourages other people, negative language has the opposite effect, so every chance you get, give someone a compliment. Everyone craves praise, and something as simple as a sincere, 'Well done!' means a lot."

People want to feel that they are important and that their views are being listened to. When you deal with someone, and it really doesn't matter who it is, your goal should be to make them feel good about themselves. Ask questions, be interested, and give your full focus to the conversation. Don't be one of those people who always looks over the shoulder of the person they're talking to in the hope that someone more interesting or (worse) more important will show up. Being mindful of the words you use and how your words make others feel is a good habit to nurture.

Being mindful of the words you hear or see in the media is also important. I wanted to make it clear to Ava that I wasn't suggesting she shouldn't watch TV, read the papers, or listen to the radio, I was simply making the point that there isn't a TV channel, newspaper, or radio station that isn't using words (or images) in a way that's designed to get you believing something that isn't necessarily true. The head of public relations at one of the largest companies in the world once told me that 90% of what you read in the press isn't true, and most of the rest isn't true in the way they have presented it. Clearly, this was the view of a very cynical person, and I don't know that I'd go quite so far, but she knew a great deal about the way journalists distort things, having been a journalist herself before she moved into PR.

Social media is even worse. You might slip into thinking that if everyone else is sharing untruths and distorted information, what difference does it make if you do the same? Well, it does make a difference, because it makes a difference to you; a difference in the way you see yourself and in how other people see you. Back in the days when forgery and clipping coins was a common way of making money at other people's expense, the situation was summed up by Gresham's Law: "Bad money drives out good." We could update those words to today's world with, "Bad (fake) news drives out good (the truth)" and we'd have a very good description of social media.

How you do something is how you do everything. Some people dabble in things – they do a bit of this, get bored, and then do a bit of that, and get bored again… You can be pretty sure that this is how they approach everything in life. Other people focus, laser-like, on accomplishing something, and you can be fairly certain that they adopt the same attitude in everything they do. If your daily behaviours are consistently low-quality, your outcomes are likely to match. Every area of your life affects every other area of your life, so when you decide to do something, always give your best. When your days are filled with only the core essentials that mean the world to you, and you're succeeding in those areas, you will absolutely dominate in all areas of your life. It's my experience that as you come closer to living daily with your good new habits, values, and ideals, amazing things start to happen. You feel happier; you're more present to those you love; you spend your time better; you pursue bigger dreams and ambitions; you're more resilient during challenges; you live at a higher frequency, and everything around you will reflect that. Soon enough, you are fully committed to being who you know you can be, and this is effectively the point of no return. Pass this point, and nothing will stop you.

I could see a puzzled look on Ava's face, the sort of look that kids sometimes have when they're thinking about arguing – not that she ever holds back when there's something on her mind. She said, "What you're telling me is that I need to focus only on what is really important to me. Well, okay, Dad, if you say so, but what about all the little things that aren't so important but still matter?"

"Give me an example."

"Okay. Let's say I go on wanting a medical career, and that's the most important thing in my mind, but it isn't the *only* thing. There's other stuff I want to do, and other stuff I want to take an interest in. I want to know what's on at the theatre. I want to know what my favourite music acts are doing, and I want to know what new acts are coming along, because sometimes my favourite acts stop being my favourite, they get displaced by something new. Am I supposed to ignore all that?"

To answer her question, I explained that it wasn't about ignoring all of that, it was more a case of concentrating on what's really important and then finding that all those other things drop into place. It's not forgetting about them or ignoring them, and you don't need to lose them. They're always there and you can turn to them in your spare moments. Those other interests are what make you a more rounded and complete person. The danger in going the other way and allowing less important things to become your central focus is that they tend to become the most important thing in your life. You then wake up one day when you're about 30 and wonder what happened to that dream you had – whether it was to become a surgeon, an anaesthetist, a consultant, a GP, or anything else. In my opinion, this is the reason why most people never fulfil their potential; their dreams remain just that – only dreams. Getting caught up in the less important bits of their lives leads to losing sight of the one important bit that they wanted to be paramount.

Having said all this, it got me thinking about my own life. If something is important to you, it becomes a "must do" rather than a "need to do" or "would like to do", and you become energised by it. You produce high quality work, you put in high quality effort, and you could say it's the difference between knowing something in your head and knowing it in your heart. I knew from my teens the benefits of a healthy lifestyle, but I played at it. I dabbled with going to the gym, eating a healthy diet, staying hydrated, meditating, being more aware, and all the other things that we as humans tend to pick up from time to time, and then put down again. However, those things stopped being a "like to do" and became a "must do" the day I got married: not because I'd suddenly gained new responsibilities, but because it was the day I was diagnosed with T1D. Since then, I've lived the lifestyle I should have been living without waiting for a diagnosis.

For this reason, I invite anyone reading these words to learn from my mistake and not wait for some form of trauma or tragedy to occur before taking action to stop dabbling in things that are simply too important to just dabble in – meaning everything connected to what you really want to do with your life. Something we all need to accept is that if we don't achieve what is within our capacity to achieve, there's no point in blaming someone else, or blaming circumstances, or the weather, or... any of the many things people commonly blame. If you don't achieve something you wanted to achieve, and were capable of achieving, the fault lies in one place only. It lies with you.

Taking Opportunities

I once spoke to a man born in the UK in the 1940s. He evidently had a good brain, having passed the 11+ and then gone to grammar school. His mother had been born in 1915, one of eight children born to a Durham miner father. She had also passed an exam that gave her entry to a grammar school, but she was unable to take it up. She had a scholarship, but it wasn't enough; her parents couldn't afford to send her to that school. From the age of 12, she was looking after the younger children in the family, and by 14 she was skivvying in a farmhouse. Her father, the miner, was described to me by the man I was talking to as the most intelligent man he'd ever met. Not academic cleverness – you need an education for that – but an intelligence that he was never able to turn into a career because at the age of 12 he'd started work down the pit, just as his father, grandfather, and brothers had done before him.

What struck me about this story was that the man telling it to me said neither his mother nor grandfather had ever expressed any bitterness about not having been able to put their above-average brains to use. It was simply the world they lived in, and the way things were. By the time he was born, the RA Butler Education Act had been passed, and when it became clear that he'd inherited his grandfather's and mother's brains, the whole family got behind him. He was going to have an education. He was going to transcend the boundaries that had previously been set. He told me that he always knew what he could do and how far he could go, and what his family had drummed into him was that it was up to him. They'd say, "It's up to you. You have the opportunity we didn't have, but only you can take it. We can't take it for you. Nobody can."

Now in his 70s, he looks back on a life in which he has, by and large, fulfilled all his ambitions. What we should all take away from his story is the lesson taught to him by his family: it's up to you. You can achieve your ambitions and have the satisfaction of knowing that you've done so, or you can fail to fulfil your potential. If it's the first, no-one can take the credit away from you. If it's the second, no-one can take the blame for you.

Lifestyle Choices

When I was young, lifestyle wasn't a word that anyone used because we didn't know we had one. Of course, we all have a lifestyle. It's the way you live, where you go, what you do, how you do what you do, and the way you feel when you're doing it. We may not have had a name for it, but our lifestyle was how we dressed, what we were driving, and the kind of entertainment we enjoyed. Your lifestyle is effectively everything about you, and even at the age of 14, I could say to Ava that her lifestyle was saying a great deal about her, communicating a clear message to others about who she is and how she thinks.

Wealth and happiness combine to create lifestyle, but it's important to understand that the wealth I'm talking about isn't measured by the amount of money you have stored away. There's a saying that your health is your wealth, and given my particular position, I understand the meaning of it very well. But it applies to everyone, not just people with a potentially fatal illness – and when you think about it, every single one of us has a fatal illness when you consider that no-one gets out of life alive. We can't change the facts of life and death, but we can have a big influence on whether we go through life being happy or sad.

In a nutshell, my message to Ava was, "If we spend more time on doughnuts than we do on books, it suggests something about the sincerity of our desire for personal progress." I think it's fair to say that most people don't study happiness and wealth, they just go through each day with their fingers crossed, hoping that something will somehow work out in a way that will make them happy. But happiness is an art, not an accident.

What I wanted to make clear to Ava was that changing how you live doesn't take more money. What it takes is deliberate thought and appreciation of the real values in life. I've met some really rich people – although not that many, because they tend to go to different places and mix in different circles to the rest of us. F Scott Fitzgerald once said, "The very rich are different from you and me," and there can be no doubt that they are. It's widely believed that Ernest Hemingway replied with, "Yes, they are – they have more money," although the reality is that these words were probably written somewhere rather than spoken. What Hemingway did say was that the rich are dull, and they drink too much. It's not for me to comment on the drinking, but I think he was right in that the few very rich people I've met didn't appear to be enjoying life. They had everything the glossy supplements in Sunday papers would have you believe you need to be happy, but what they didn't have was a sense of pleasure in having those things. I think this is perhaps what marks out the very rich most clearly; it doesn't matter how much they have, they want more.

"So, let's not do that," I said to Ava. "Instead, let's find the things that give us the greatest enjoyment and do those. If your experience is anything like mine, you'll find that those things don't cost a lot of money. It might be finding the coffee shop you really like to visit, finding the people you most want to spend time with, the places you like to walk, the places you most want to explore next, the something you really quite like to eat… and you do those things. See those people, walk there, go there and look around, and find somewhere that serves the something you want to eat. It won't always work. I spent my childhood years in South Africa, and I used to eat a lot of foods that you can't always find in other countries. Special kinds of sausages, things like that, and you haven't really seen a barbecue until you've seen how the South Africans do them, though we call a barbecue a braai. There's a fish (actually a type of eel) in South Africa called kingklip. You can find it in parts of South America, but you can't find it anywhere else, and even in South Africa it's not available all year round. You can't buy it at all in England, or if you can, I've never found it. Believe me, I've looked, because kingklip is possibly the most delicious fish you can eat. So, I do sometimes hanker after a plate of kingklip – grill it or fry it, squeeze some lemon juice over it (or lime juice, whichever you prefer), serve it with salad and (if you must) a small portion of chips (fries in South Africa) – and once you taste it, you'll know you're eating what they eat in heaven. The point I'm making is that kingklip isn't hugely expensive, and the occasional trip to South Africa isn't beyond the means of anyone who works towards that goal. It isn't what the glossy magazines tell you to aspire to or strive for, and you may think you'd rather go to Mustique and mix with aristocrats, but the latter is a dream that, once achieved, is unlikely to inspire a return visit.

"You'll quickly realise that you're surrounded by people who have lots of money and a very high opinion of themselves (and a low opinion of anyone who doesn't have piles of money), but they'd bore any intelligent person to tears because they have no conversation, and in the grand scale of things they know nothing worth knowing. As Oscar Wilde once put it, they know the price of everything and the value of nothing."

What I wanted Ava to understand through all of this was that lifestyle isn't about money; it's about things that make you happy.

Building Healthy Habits

Being healthy means different things to different people at different stages in their lives, but no matter who you are or how old you are, eating a balanced diet, getting regular exercise, and maintaining good hygiene are all important factors of health. Having a positive mental attitude is also important, so that you can make safe decisions about your body and behaviours. In short, being healthy allows you to feel confident, look great, and keep your body in good working order!

When it comes to eating healthily, it's really a matter of making good food choices. It's not as clear cut as "good" foods versus "bad" foods, it's all about moderation. You can have the occasional lapse – a quarter pounder with cheese and fries from McDonald's can be an occasional indulgence that won't do any harm, but *occasional* is the key word here. What you eat is not only fuel for your body, but also for your brain. I needed Ava to know that I wasn't about to lay down rules on what should or shouldn't be eaten, because even the nutritional experts studying the subject are prone to changing their minds. What this suggests is that there are perhaps as many unknowns as there are knowns, and even the experts can't know what they don't know.

When I was young, we were told to stay away from shrimps, prawns, and shelled seafood in general, because they were high in cholesterol and would block our arteries. Today, the advice is that these foods will do us no harm. The same is true of dairy fats. Until recently, they were considered things we should avoid, and now we're told they're not responsible for all the heart problems that used to be associated with them. However, we do know that fresh fruits and vegetables are good for us, as are whole grains, nuts, beans, peas, and lentils, along with fish and chicken for non-vegetarians. So my advice to Ava was to stick with those choices for the most part, and then having the occasional dive into something that makes you feel good isn't going to cause harm – in moderation. I had no choice. Once I was diagnosed with Type I Diabetes, I had to learn how to count calories in order to keep control of my blood sugars. I had to learn the glycaemic levels of foods, and I had to know and understand my

BMI (Body Mass Index) level, but healthy diets aren't just for people like me. Eating healthily benefits everyone.

Nutrition is a huge subject, and it's known that eating disorders occur all too frequently in teenagers (boys as well as girls), so I didn't want Ava to get bogged down in it. I said, "Most people, if they are going to skip a meal, will skip breakfast. Don't do that. Breakfast provides your body with its first fuel of the day, and this is going to help you concentrate. Then, instead of buying lunch at school, think about packing your own lunch to take with you. That way, you get two good things: you know you're going to eat something you want to eat, and you know it will be good for you."

Eat plenty. In my opinion, one of the worst things to have happened in relation to the way people eat over the course of the last 50 years or so has been the "invention" of fad and crash diets. Yes, you can lose weight that way, but you'll put it all back on. My advice to Ava at this point was, "If you're concerned about your weight, try smaller plates. Or, as the plates we have at home are all the same size, put less on them. But you do need a minimum level of calories. The average teenage girl who isn't very active needs an absolute minimum of 1600 calories a day. The same girl, if she plays a lot of sport, probably needs 2400. But don't focus on how much you weigh, instead, find out your BMI because it's going to give you a better understanding of whether you are a healthy weight for your age and height."

Drink plenty. Dehydration has a negative impact on everything, both body and brain function, so drink plenty of water. Carry a reusable water bottle that you can fill from the tap throughout the day, and if you need a little extra flavour to encourage regular hydration habits, try adding a slice of fresh lemon or lime (just be sure to keep your water and your slices fresh each day).

Sleep plenty. Most teenagers need around 8-10 hours of sleep every night to get the most out of their day. If you're not sleeping enough, you lose focus, your attention wanders, and you get into bad moods. Without enough sleep, you're probably going to struggle to get up in the morning, you might fall asleep in class, you're going to struggle to maintain concentration, and it could lead to mood swings or feelings of depression. Getting more sleep can be a simple case of setting a regular bedtime for yourself, or perhaps cutting back on the amount of caffeine you consume after a certain time in the afternoon. Pulling an all-nighter might seem fun at the time, but it can play havoc with your sleep schedule for days.

And exercise regularly. A daily exercise habit would be ideal, but getting some form of exercise at least three to five times, every week is a sensible target. Exercise boosts your energy levels, helps you feel good, and reduces stress. Try to work up a sweat – or get your breathing rate up to the point that you'd need to shorten your sentences if you were talking – for at least 20-30 minutes, preferably up to an hour. Aerobic exercises such as brisk walking, jogging, cycling, or swimming get your heart pumping and your breathing rate up, and they're great for your heart health and overall wellbeing.

More specific workouts can target areas of your body you want to focus on, such as strengthening your legs or your core muscles. Maintaining good posture can be a challenge for a lot of young people. Not wanting to be noticed can lead to shrinking into themselves, but in fact, learning to "walk tall" with good posture not only improves muscle strength, but it also helps to build self-esteem.

Staying Mentally Healthy

All of the above are important factors of physical health, but it's equally important to look after your mental health. The list of things that can contribute to mental health problems is very long. It's easy to lump mental health issues in with drug abuse or a family history of mental illness, but this is not the case. Causes are numerous, and include loneliness, continuous stress, job loss, or bereavement, to name just a few. There are some situations you can't control, but one thing everyone can do is adopt a positive attitude. Something else that can really help is simply to understand that

your mental health and habits are for you and your wellbeing, not for anyone else's benefit. Avoid getting dragged into the opinions of others; know yourself, and know what makes you feel healthy and good about yourself. Being yourself and believing in yourself is a positive way to stay mentally healthy.

Ava said that she'd never considered herself to have poor mental health. I agreed, saying, "I think your mental state is pretty damn good, and if you keep your positive attitude and go on thinking positive thoughts, it should stay that way. What you tell yourself in your head can really affect how you feel and how you perceive the world around you. You'll make mistakes, of course, we all do, and you wouldn't be human if you didn't, but some people get really down on themselves when mistakes are made. There's never any need to give yourself a hard time or to think 'I'm such a loser' thoughts when all a mistake does is confirm that you're human. All that's needed is to pick yourself up and carry on."

One of my favourite books is called *The Hidden Messages in Water*. It's an eye-opening theory about water's deep connection to people's individual and collective consciousness. Drawing from his own discoveries, the author describes the ability of water to absorb, hold, and even retransmit human feelings and emotions. Using high-speed photography, he found that crystals formed in ice reveal changes when specific, concentrated thoughts are directed towards it. Music, visual images, words written on paper, and photographs were all shown to have an impact on the crystal structure.

The author theorises that since water can receive a wide range of frequencies, it can also reflect the universe in this manner. He found that water from clear springs and water exposed to loving words shows brilliant, complex, and colourful snowflake patterns, while polluted water and water exposed to negative thoughts forms incomplete, distorted patterns with dull colours. Adult human beings are around 60 per cent water, but the brain and heart are around 70 per cent water

– which, as it happens, is the same as the percentage of water on the Earth's surface. The book suggests that we can heal our planet and ourselves by consciously expressing love and goodwill. Now, I don't know how widely or well received the author's theories have been, but from my own experience, I do believe that speaking to and about myself in a positive way helps with my own mental health.

Something else I wanted Ava to know was that avoiding comparison with others is another way to help improve your mental health. Comparison is the death of joy. It's fine to think about someone who does something better than you do, so long as you restrict yourself to admiring that person and thinking about what you could do to become better at whatever it is. Not better than the other person, just better than you currently are. I said, "Comparison is closely linked to envy, which can not only get you down, but it can also prevent you from remembering all the things that make you amazing.

"Don't believe that everyone on the internet is as happy as they seem. Sure, everyone on Facebook and Twitter seems to have an amazing, glamorous life, but the reality is that everyone has problems and struggles. Anyone pretending otherwise probably isn't as happy as they try to make themselves appear, especially when they're in their teens. I was a teenager once, and I remember what it can be like."

My advice to Ava was to express herself creatively. Journaling, music, art, anything that would let her express herself in a creative way. This is good advice for anyone, as it can help to reduce stress, teach you to value your positive attributes, and give you a feeling of accomplishment. I suggested experimenting with more hobbies and skills, and to always keep in mind that being naturally "talented" isn't what matters; it's all about just doing things for you, whether you're good at it or not, and irrespective of what anyone else thinks. I know someone who sings when he is happy – and his singing is appalling! He spent a great deal of time in South Wales and, as you may know, Wales is a nation renowned for great singers. Whenever he started singing there, they'd plead with him to stop, but he sings when he's happy. It's not for anyone else, so who can deny him that?

Everyone can do something creative. Perhaps learn to play a musical instrument, draw, paint, craft, or build something. Most children are creative when they're young, but many don't carry that creativity forward into their teenage years or adult life because they're afraid they're not good enough. To make things worse, they may have been told they're not good enough by their peers, teachers, or even their parents. The message I want to get across is that it doesn't matter. If, for example, you like to write, then write. Maybe you'll send what you've written to a publisher who writes back, saying, "Have you thought of taking up knitting?" It doesn't matter. You weren't writing with the sole purpose of selling your work; you were writing to improve your mental health. You have enjoyed being creative, so you have only gained through the process.

To Ava, I said, "Know that you are beautiful, and know that this is true no matter how you look. The way you view your physical self is closely linked to your self-esteem, so having a positive body image is extremely important for you as a teen, since you might feel pressured by peers or media to look different than you do. Work on having a positive body image and remember that your body is your own, no matter what it looks like. This is your vessel for an exciting life. Treat it with respect and appreciate it for all its uniqueness. Recognise which elements of your appearance you can change, and which you can't. Let go of the things you can't change. Remember that everyone has something about themselves they don't like very much. Setting yourself goals to change things you *can* change is a positive way to work on improving your mental health. If you want to lose weight, create a healthy diet and exercise plan. If you feel your hair is boring, experiment with a new cut. Compliment yourself every day. It might sound silly, but tell yourself something nice every day, and mean what you say."

Develop Time Management Skills

Between school, homework, friends, family, work, personal time, and anything else you might have going on, there's a lot to juggle in life. Developing time management skills helps you to get everything you need to get done, done, without feeling overwhelmed in the process. "Making a to-do list for the week works for me," I explained to Ava. "I break up big tasks into smaller tasks, and I get ready for the following day the night before so that I don't find myself scrambling in the morning and potentially forgetting something." I also told her that keeping things physically organised by having a place for everything makes it much harder to lose things, but this is not a concept that many teenagers are able to grasp!

Stress

Stress is a strange thing. You need a certain amount of it in your life, but too much can lead to physical illness, and it could even kill you by causing a heart attack. Even at low level, prolonged stress can lead to serious mental health issues. If you feel on edge, tired, depressed, or guilty, stress might be at the root of it. Headaches, stomach trouble, inability to sleep well, negative thoughts, loss of enjoyment in things you used to like doing, resentment – all of these are possible indicators of stress.

I said to Ava, "To be able to deal with your stress levels, you need to identify where the stress is coming from. Consciously make a note of the things that are stressing you out, then divide those things into things you can control and things you can't. Accept the things you can't change. Acceptance alone will greatly reduce the stress those things create. As for the things you *can* change, begin to make changes where you can. It's not going to be possible to change everything all at once, but the process of beginning to make small, manageable changes paves the way for taking control over bigger changes.

"Sometimes you're just too busy, leading to feelings of never being able to get everything you need to do done. When this is the case, you need to decide which activity is the least important in your life and then stop doing it. The time this creates can go a long way towards alleviating stress, but it's something you may need to repeat – you may need to drop the next least important activity on the list a few more times to reach a point where you feel you've got your time management under control. Saying no to doing things you don't want to do, or you already know you don't have time to do, will also minimise stress. Helping others is great, but not if it interferes with your own wellbeing. Perhaps most importantly of all, talking about the way you're feeling really helps. If you can't talk to your mother and me, talk to someone else, whether it's a friend, another family member, a counsellor, or anyone else."

Journaling is something I've found to be very helpful in terms of venting frustrations. It's a habit I only adopted later in life, and I wish I'd known about the benefits of it when I was a teenager. A lot of teens feel they can't speak to anyone about their struggles, and this is where writing in a journal can help. Writing down whatever is on your mind gives you an opportunity to reflect on your relationships and experiences, and it also provides a place to consider who you are and who you want to be. As well as recording frustrations, recording all the good things you have in your life can really help you to keep things in perspective. You might be surprised by just how blessed you really are when you open your eyes and mind to see things differently. A journal is for your eyes only, no-one else ever needs to know what you're writing in there, so you have total freedom to offload every thought that crosses your mind.

Self-Esteem

Something I've discovered to be true is that trying new things can really help boost your mental health and self-esteem. Little victories are steppingstones to greater self-esteem, and no victory is too small. It might even be something no-one else notices, such as cooking a dish you've never cooked before, or reading a book from cover to cover. It can be the victory of successfully finishing any small task. It doesn't need to be anything huge; it's simply the feeling of having achieved something you haven't done before. Whenever the opportunity arises to do something interesting that you've never tried before, seize it! Experiencing new and different activities will not only make you a more balanced person, it will also get you into the habit of becoming a life-long learner.

To back up my point, I said to Ava, "School, college, and university are all good and necessary ways to get a traditional education – but they are not the only ones. Life is full of learning experiences. You should do your best at school, but don't leave it there. Sometimes people are afraid to ask about things because they fear they might be asking a 'stupid question', but questions are never stupid (although some answers might be) and getting help or advice from someone who knows more about something than you do can never be a bad idea. Learning helps to build your self-esteem and being seen as someone who is willing to learn makes you someone others enjoy spending time with – and this is also great for building self-esteem.

"People look up to smart, active people in the community, and being well regarded makes you feel better about yourself. Read as much as you can. You know I'm an avid reader, and I would much rather read a good book than watch TV. It's said that reading a book is like having a conversation with the author, and I love that. I'm having conversations with people that I look up to, be they alive or dead. Books are experiences in permanent form. It doesn't matter what you choose to read, whether it's a bestseller, classic literature, how-to manual, self-help book, or even stuff you don't agree with; it's all learning.

"One of the most worrying developments in the last 20 years is the way the art of debate has disappeared. Here we are in a world where so much can go wrong, and it seems that a large chunk of the population has decided to not even listen to the points of view of anyone with an opinion that's different to theirs. If you read something you don't agree with, examine it. Are you sure that what you've read is 100% wrong and you are 100% right? What evidence do you have for that? And is it really evidence, or does it actually amount to bias?"

I spent a long time earlier in my life trying to work out whether I had any special talent. I know Ava has some – playing the guitar, painting, cooking, fashion design – but when you're young and you're aware that you're not going to get an academic certificate for any of those activities, it's easy to decide you really don't have time for that interest right now and that you need to focus on school or college work. It's easy, but it's a mistake. My advice to Ava is to keep on taking 15 to 30 minutes out of every day to work on something she knows she's good at and something she really enjoys, but to also make sure she's still having fun doing it. In so doing, she's going to be building her self-confidence, and she's going to find that new opportunities for fun will spring up from taking part in those activities.

Over the years, I've always advised Ava to make an extra effort to get to know other people in her world. The reason for this has simply been wanting her to learn about others and to enjoy finding out about them, talking to them, and making them (rather than herself) the subject of conversation. The better we understand others, the better we will understand ourselves, and knowing yourself is at the heart of learning to manage your mental health. Beauty is all around, and it's often said that beauty is in the eye of the beholder.

It's also said that everyone is beautiful in their own way, but this is something that can be hard to accept, and we need to learn to be supportive of other people's processes. Everyone needs help at some point in their life, and then when it's our turn, people will repay kindness with kindness. I hate to see people put others down, telling them they're stupid, saying something negative about them, or drawing attention to their flaws. I don't understand why people feel the need to do it when everyone has flaws, not least themselves. Learning to recognise the positive things in others helps all of us to appreciate and develop them in ourselves.

As a parent of teenage children, it's a good idea to remember how it felt to be a teenager yourself. Sometimes, if we're entirely honest about our memories, we went out of our way to disobey our parents and anyone else in authority. And, while we may occasionally have come across adults who didn't want the best for us, those adults were never our parents and rarely our teachers. Most adults, when they gave advice, gave it from a position of having been through the same experiences themselves. Today's teens are not going to avoid every mistake their elders made, but if they listen, they can often find that the advice they're getting is good.

It's a matter of common sense, but the problem with common sense is that it's by no means common. If it were, would we even have the worry of teenagers taking up drugs, alcohol, or cigarettes? Perhaps I'm being hopelessly optimistic, and maybe it's time to remind myself to be realistic.

Be Realistic

The Book of Proverbs says, *"Wisdom is with the modest ones."* Modest people are realistic. They realise that there are limits to their time, their energy, and the resources they have available, so they don't give in to the temptation to change every aspect of their lives immediately.

It's easy to tell yourself that this week you will stop eating junk food, go to bed at a reasonable time, *and* start exercising, but what experience tells us is that trying to reach all your goals at the same time is a sure way to reach none of them. The modest person, the one Proverbs tells us has wisdom, doesn't try to change everything at once. They make improvements gradually.

I explained this to Ava by saying, "You can work on your habits in realistic increments. Lists are a good idea for lots of things, and here we need two: a list of good habits that you would like to build; and a list of bad habits that you need to get rid of. You don't need to make it a short list, you can just write down as many good or bad habits as you can think of, and then number them in order of importance to you. That's how you set your priorities. You then choose one or two habits from the top of each list and make those the ones you'll focus on this week. And, if necessary, next week and the week after that, simply keeping it going until you're satisfied that the good ones are now strong, and you've got rid of the bad ones.

"From there, you move on to the next one or two habits on each of your lists. If you make it your aim to create a new habit in 30 days, a year from now you'll have 12 good new habits. You have to admit, that's pretty amazing."

End of Day Three

There's a glacier lagoon in Southeast Iceland and it's filled with icebergs. A deep, inky lake set against a backdrop of snow-capped peaks and littered with icebergs of all shapes and sizes, Jökulsárlón is one of Iceland's most compelling destinations, and its stunning beauty has made this ice lagoon one of the country's most popular attractions.

Jökulsárlón means Glacier's-River-Lagoon. It's at the southern edge of the Vatnajökull glacier and it's regarded as one of Iceland's greatest natural wonders. Huge chunks of ice regularly calve off the glacier and make their way through the lagoon into the sea, and because the ice chunks lying on it look like diamonds glistening in the sun, Icelanders call the nearby black beach the Diamond Beach. Sadly, the glacier is rapidly receding, and the lake is increasing in size as the meltwater descends. It now covers a huge area at the foot of the mountains.

Many of the bergs are striped with frozen layers of black volcanic ash, and others are perfectly white or tinged with blue. Over time, they melt and re-freeze, topple and turn, providing an endless variety of views. Hollywood loves this scene, and the lake has featured in many films, including *Lara Croft: Tomb Raider*, *Batman Begins*, and two James Bond movies, *A View to Kill* and *Die Another Day*.

I really believe it's a place to visit and a view to be witnessed in person at least once in your life, and it has been the highlight of our trip so far.

Chapter 5
Your Tribe Is Your Vibe

"Choose your friends wisely. Association is perception. Perception is reality." – Unknown

Day 4: East Fjords, Djupivogur and Mývatn

After yesterday's exertions, we decided to take it a little easier today. Most of the day was going to be spent driving, but we wanted to take our time driving along the east coast and pull over to whatever caught our eye. We also planned to stop by Detifoss, but the first road we tried was closed off due to snow, so we decided to skip that waterfall. It wasn't the loss it might have been, because we had already seen plenty of waterfalls and planned on visiting Godafoss the next day.

We pulled over at a couple of spots where we could get near to the ocean, and stopped by Djupivogur to get some food and petrol. It's a cute little town with a population of only 470. We ate at the Vio Vogin restaurant and ordered pylsurs (hot dogs) and coffee. We loved the hot dogs in Iceland. In my case, especially with added fried onions and remoulade sauce. Our next pit stop was Egilsstaoir, a little town with a population of 2100 people.

We were driving on gravel roads up the side of mountains, so things got a bit scary at times, especially when there seemed to be a lack of barriers to prevent us from plunging over the edge. Some of those drops were a long way down – and then it started to snow. When we hadn't seen another car for an hour, I was about ready to freak out, but then we were on top of a mountain, we were on paved roads, and suddenly all felt well once more. Stunning views, fresh, untouched snow all around us, and as if that were not enough, the sun broke through the low-hanging clouds.

Power by Association

I'd been concentrating on driving, but now we were both able to relax and Ava raised a subject that had obviously been on her mind. She'd been finding things a bit tough lately, saying, "A friend, who I thought was my good friend, has done and said things that have made me quite sad. I'm not sure what to do."

I understood what she was saying, because I'd been through the same sort of thing myself at her age. I imagine most people in their teens do.

Good friendships are important for us to be happy. I knew Ava as a very sociable person, but I also knew she was sensitive, so I understood the sadness she might feel when a friend, especially a good friend, said or did something that didn't sit right with her. So, what do you say in a situation like that? Well, what I said was, "You know, friendships can be tricky. They don't just go on automatically; they demand effort. But good friendships are always worth it, and one of the things we have to remember is that we and our friends are not joined at the hip. They have their lives, and we have ours. What seems important to one of us might be less so to the other. The worst case is when someone who has been our friend decides they don't want to play that role any longer. That can get vicious. But, usually, when one of you says or does something that upsets the other person, you can work it out."

Ava was quick to defend herself by pointing out that she was talking about something her friend had been doing, not her. I knew this, but I wanted her to consider for a moment if it was possible that her friend at some point may have had the same discussion with her parents about something Ava had said or done. After giving it some thought, she came to realise that it wasn't impossible, but she still wanted to know what she should do.

To answer her question, I said, "You talk to her. If you really want to know how to make a mess of something like this, go about it when you're in a bad temper, or feeling defensive. Instead, make sure you're feeling calm before you do it. Tell her how you're feeling and invite her to do the same. If you're really good friends, she'll be glad to know what's bothering you and she'll also be glad to tell you what's bothering her. And, if the friendship has served its term and isn't a real friendship any longer, you'll find out."

Ava's response to this suggestion was, "That sounds a bit risky, and it sounds a bit difficult... just walking up to someone and saying, 'I want to tell you why I'm upset.' Isn't that asking for trouble?"

"Maybe," I said, "but *not* doing it is almost certainly asking for trouble. If you don't deal with a problem, it doesn't go away, it gets worse. It's part of being human that you or your friend will sometimes say and do things that might upset the other person. But good friends always work things out – by apologising, talking things out, and seeing the other person's point of view."

I thought this was good advice, but then I found that it wasn't quite as straightforward as it had seemed. This had happened between Ava and her friend before. Ava had done what I'd suggested, telling her friend that she was upset and telling her why, but the friend was still doing it. It was now clear that we were dealing with a different kind of problem, so I said, "When you're young, losing a friend seems disastrous, and it's sometimes because you don't have a great many real friends, meaning losing one feels like a big loss."

This led Ava to question why it would be any different when she was older. I could understand why she'd question this, and it highlighted that as a teenager, you're perhaps not ready to hear that friends will come and go in life. I explained, "Some people in their 60s and 70s are still in touch with people they knew when they were at school, but generally very few. Most people are like me, no longer in contact with anyone from their school days, even though they seemed so close and important back then. I went off to university and made new friends, and they went off on their own life trajectories, some into jobs and some to other universities, where they also made new friends. Like me, many of them have probably moved several times in their lives, for work or for other reasons, and they've left behind the friends they'd made wherever they were and made new ones in their new location."

This made me think of someone I'd met a couple of times. He told me that he'd grown up in a different part of England, and even though he'd moved a long time ago, he still went back to his old hometown once a year to have dinner with two guys he was at school with. He knows exactly why he does it. All three of them were athletes. One played football; one played rugby, cricket, and was a distance runner; and one played football and cricket. Each time they meet, it's like they're taking up the conversation again as if they only left off yesterday, although it has in fact been a year. Of course, what's really happening is that three old men, who can no longer even run for a bus, are remembering what it was like to be fit and in training, and to have a body that obeyed them instinctively. They are reliving what is gone, but they're still a minority. There were 120 boys in their year at school, and only the three of them have kept in touch, as far as they know. They have no idea what became of the other 117, and it just goes to show that most friendships are fairly short term.

Thinking about this got me pondering over a popular saying: *"Show me who your friends are, and I'll tell you who you are."* The wisdom in this saying was also passed on by legendary personal development coach Jim Rohn when he said, *"You are the average of the five people you spend the most time with."* You see, your friends really define you. They can bring out the best in you and have a positive impact in your life, or they can bring you down and have a negative impact in your life. Later in life, I realised that the less you associate with unpleasant people, the more your life will improve. A lesson there for Ava? Perhaps. But deciding not to associate with unpleasant people isn't always easy, and it wasn't something I'd always done. We talk about a young person getting in with the wrong crowd, and sometimes the people I associated with when I was young got me into trouble. It affected my relationship with the people who loved and cared for me most, but at that stage in my life, I didn't care about that.

The only thing I cared about was being in with what I thought was the cool crowd, and rules did not apply to them. One example of this was asking my grandad if I could borrow his car to go to a friend's house. I was 16 at the time, and I didn't go to a friend's. I picked up loads of friends and we went to Johannesburg nightclubs. I didn't have a driver's licence, the car was seriously overloaded, and we almost got into a big accident due to driving too fast and weaving all over the road. We laughed about it at the time. It felt cool. It's only later that you realise just how bad the consequences could have been.

Being in trouble for breaking the law would have been the least of it. There are times when you read a newspaper account of a trial for something that caused someone's death, and the defending counsel says, "My client will have to live with this for the rest of his life." I don't want to be that person; the one who lives with something for the rest of his life, especially if the something I'm living with is the fact that someone's life was cut short by my actions. I didn't understand that then. I understand it now.

I learned. My definition of what is cool changed, and while it's true that my friends were a bad influence on me, I had to accept that I was probably a bad influence on them. Acceptance is growth. Stuff I went through when I was young eventually taught me that tolerating mediocrity in others increases your own mediocrity. I learned later in life that an important attribute in successful people is their impatience with negative thinking and negative people. As I started to grow, my associations changed.

In telling Ava this, I said, "I think you'll have the same experience. Some of your friends will not want you to grow. They'll want you to stay where they are. Friends who don't help you climb will want you to crawl, but know from my experience that your real friends will stretch your vision and not limit your dreams. Associations that don't increase you will eventually decrease you."

Something I once read amused me: *If you want to know how you can ever afford a Bentley, advice from someone driving a Toyota is best ignored.* This made me smile, but it's very true in that you should never discuss your problems, or dreams for that matter, with someone who can't contribute to the solutions. Those who never succeed themselves are always first to tell you how. Something we hear a lot more today than we used to is that everyone is entitled to respect. I'm not going to dispute that, but I will suggest that you need to examine exactly what kind of respect you're going to give.

Not everyone has the right to speak in your life. Exchange ideas with the wrong person and you can be quite sure you're getting the worst of the bargain. Don't follow anyone who's going nowhere. This doesn't mean that you don't show them respect. Every human being *is* entitled to respect, but not every opinion is good, and not all opinions are worthy of your attention. Some opinions are best ignored, but not in such a way that it will hurt the other person's feelings. Knowingly hurting someone's feelings is not showing them respect.

Something I've believed for a long time is that regret is a corrosive emotion and best avoided. I said to Ava, "You're 14; you have your whole life ahead of you. You *will* make mistakes, and if you choose to get hung up on them and feel down every time you realise you've made one, you'll be punishing yourself unnecessarily. Instead, what you need to do when you make a mistake is to learn from it and move on. Learning from it is key. Doing something that other people might consider a silly thing to have done is not in itself silly. What *is* silly is doing the same thing again, repeating the mistake, and expecting it to turn out differently. Don't do that. If you make a mistake, think of it as a learning opportunity, and move on from it knowing it's now something you won't do again."

Choose Wisely

Something Ava had picked up from everything I'd been saying was that we should choose our friends wisely. This got us into a bit of a discussion, because she wanted to know how to do that and asked what she should be looking out for – a question that's easier to ask than to answer.

I could think of lots of quotes on the subject. Wise words such as, "Run with wolves and you'll learn how to howl," or, "Associate with eagles and you'll soar to great heights," for example. But as inspiring as these words may be, they don't actually answer Ava's question, or explain what it means to run with wolves or soar with eagles. The message I wanted to get across to her was that being around aspirational people would help her to become the best version of her it was possible to be.

I explained by saying, "The most important thing is to try to be around people who are what we want to be. Over time, we come to dress, think, talk, and act like the people we surround ourselves with, and that's not something that should be left to chance. If you want the best chance of succeeding, take a look at your associations. You need to look for people who will support you on your journey to success; people on a similar success journey themselves, or who have already achieved what you want to achieve. These might be people that read the right books, hang out in the right places, and share your beliefs, and these are the people you need to actively invest your time in and become friends with. It's easy to imagine that we have some kind of obligation to be friendly with anyone who makes overtures of friendship towards us, but this isn't true. No such obligation exists. In fact, when you come right down to it, the real obligation is to yourself, and it's to not accept any friendship that has the potential to prevent you from reaching your goals."

I suggested that she should think about what those goals are, then ask herself a couple of questions: Will this person who seems to want to be my friend help me reach those goals? Will he or she be a neutral influence on the matter? Or will they actually get in the way?

Having said this, I then needed to add that if someone makes you feel good, then be friends with them, as long as you're happy about what it is they do to make you feel that way.

Something that successful people have in common is that they're surrounded by other successful people. This isn't an accident. They don't become successful one day and then find other successful people to invite into their world. They invite other successful people, or people on a journey similar to theirs, to join them before they ever get there. This mutual support is one of the key reasons they become successful in the first place. Almost all my successes in life are down to the mastermind groups I established in the areas I wanted to succeed in. In Proverbs, it says that whoever walks with the wise becomes wise, so a mastermind group can be a group of like-minded people or friends, existing or new, who want to succeed in the areas that you want to succeed in. The idea is that together, through learning from and supporting each other, you stand a greater chance of reaching your goals.

A writer friend once said to me, "Writers are the most unclubbable people you can imagine. We spend our lives sitting alone at a typewriter or a keyboard, interfering in the lives of people who don't exist. If we are completely honest, we don't like other people all that much, and that includes other writers." And yet, any time you speak to one of us, you'll hear us mention something another writer has said in conversation, or talk about a friend who is also a writer… so it would seem that we are quite clubbable after all. Most belong to at least one writers' group, and a trip to a literary festival isn't just to promote our books, it's to be in touch with other writers. Talking to other writers, listening to what they have to say, hearing what the latest trends are, which publishers are looking for new talent, and which editor has moved from one firm to another. This isn't something that's exclusive to writers, and I wanted Ava to know that she could do it herself by mixing with like-minded people who are following the same goals as herself.

I added, "And don't consider yourself limited to one mastermind group. I have a few groups that I tap into to help me in areas of business, or fitness and health, or building my faith, and so on. These groups have helped me immensely, and I hope that I have contributed a little to their successes as well. The same can be true for you, and people who can become your new friends are out there. You just need to work out what it is you want to focus on, and then go out and find the people who are going to be your friends as you focus on those things."

Taking Action

Never one to be slow in following up, Ava's instant response to all of this was, "Okay, so I decide what I want to do, I decide who's going to be able to help me (apart from you and Mum, of course), then what? What happens next?"

This was an excellent question, and I answered it by saying that you need to take it one step at a time. All you can do is try to make the best decisions for you at the time you make them. In my own experience, once I started associating with the right people – people who were having a positive impact on me in terms of reaching my goals – I took what I called my "three Rs" approach. This is Remove, Reduce, and Revitalise:

- **Remove certain people from your life completely.**
  There will always be people in your life who hold you back, encourage behaviour that saps your energy, or act as a bad influence in some other way that gets in the way of your success. It sounds harsh, but if you want to progress in life, you should eliminate these people from your life completely. If you don't, and you go on surrounding yourself with people who are subconsciously hostile towards your success or who aren't supportive of you on your journey to success, you will constantly be dragged away from your path and struggle to achieve anything meaningful. So, remove these people from your life. Show some tough love, and keep in mind that the best kind of tough love is tough love for yourself.

- **Reduce the time you spend with some.**
  If there are people who neither support nor discourage you, but are not on a similar success journey to yours, cut back the amount of time you

spend with them. Time is the most valuable possession you have, because it's the one thing you can never under any circumstances get back. Use it wisely and don't waste it around people who can't support you and your vision.

- **Revitalise your time with people who positively impact your life.**
  The kind of people who will support you in your vision are easily identified. They have either already achieved the level of success you desire, or they are on a journey similar to your own. These are the people you want to invest the most time with and make friends with. Revitalise your relationships with supportive and encouraging people who want to see you succeed.

Your Reputation

The people you surround yourself with will give tell-tale signs to others about what your values are and what you stand for. We've all heard of the concept of being guilty by association and the saying that birds of a feather flock together, and these highlight the fact that the company you keep reflects your personality. There's a poem that always makes me smile. Nobody knows who first wrote it or where it came from, although some believe it may be an old Irish folk song. It goes like this:

> It was a year ago, September
> A day I well remember
> I was walking up and down
> In drunken pride

When my knees began to flutter
And I fell down in the gutter
And a pig came by and lay down by my side.

As I lay there in the gutter
Thinking thoughts I could not utter
I thought I heard a passing lady say,
"You can tell a man who boozes
By the company he chooses..."
And with that, the pig got up and walked away.

After reciting it to Ava, I added, "What makes me laugh whenever I hear it is the idea that you can get yourself into such a state that even a pig won't stand for it. For most of us, that's never going to be reality, but a smart person surrounds herself with other smart people. If one of your friends acts in a negative way, you will be lumped in with her."

Whether we like it or not, people today believe what they see. People will judge you not just by what you do but according to what those closest to you do. They assume that people who are similar will spend time together. While you may be better behaved than the company you keep, having disreputable friends sends a signal to those who don't know you well enough. However much you may believe yourself to be a strong person with good thoughts and habits, a time may come when your bad company starts to influence your good behaviour.

I said to Ava, "Of course, you should lead your own life, but you should never forget that your name is your most valuable asset, and your reputation will walk with you throughout your life. There's an old proverb: 'Give a dog a bad name and hang him.' What this means is that the reputation someone has is likely to be acted out in that person's life. Your reputation can be made or broken by the company you keep.

"People are quick to judge, so you should choose your friends and companions carefully. If a person has a bad company of friends, other people may avoid them because of the image portrayed by the bad company. In your teens, you'll find that your beliefs and goals are constantly changing. You need people around you who will help you and not detract from your life. Associating with the right people brings out the best in us. It isn't what you believe that makes you a good person; it's how you behave. When you surround yourself with other people, you are exposed to their personal values, behaviours, and ideals, so it should come as no surprise if you end up taking on some of their mentality and behaviour."

This applies to all of us. If you take a close look at your five closest friends, you'll see that they are who you are. If you're happy with being that person, fine – but, if you're not, is it time to create some distance between yourself and them? It isn't about people being good or bad, or right or wrong. It's about people choosing to evolve or to remain complacent – or, even worse, go backwards. Choose those who choose to evolve. The circle of friends I have now is very different from my past circle of friends, and my life today is very different from my past life. This is not a coincidence.

Constructive Criticism

"Something else friends do for us is criticise." When I said this to Ava, she wondered how criticism could ever be a good thing, so I made sure she understood that I meant constructive criticism, not the damaging kind. People criticise others for different reasons. Some do it to make themselves feel good at the expense of the person being criticised, and when this is the case, the only thing to do is to ignore them. Others are offering criticism as advice. Think of a sports coach who knows he has a real prospect on his hands, but the prospect is still raw, inexperienced, and hasn't been through enough to see what can go wrong and how to avoid it. The advice that coach offers is constructive criticism, all aimed at helping an athlete to realise their potential.

Real friends will do the same, offering advice when they see us doing something that they think will hold us back. Of course, when constructive criticism is offered, you need to ask yourself whether the person giving it is sufficiently knowledgeable in what they have to say. If not, smile and thank them for the trouble they've taken to advise you, but carry on as before. If they *do* know what they're talking about, then any criticism can be taken seriously because constructive criticism is advice that's intended to help you – not cut you down to size.

It's also important not to take it personally. This can be difficult because no-one likes being criticised, and it's certainly something I had to learn. When I had just started work, I thought I was great at everything – anything anyone else could do, I could do better was the way I saw things. When you think you're great at everything, any criticism feels like a personal attack, even when it's the well-intended constructive variety. It took a little bit of growing up before I was able to see and accept that I wasn't great at everything and that the constructive criticism I'd been given wasn't personal, it was intended to be helpful. For example, I am good with numbers and I write a great report, but I find dealing with difficult people challenging. I've always been thankful that someone I respected pointed this out to me, and accepting it as constructive criticism meant I could use it as an opportunity to improve rather than be offended by it.

When people can share feedback and constructive criticism, everyone wins. With feedback, we can learn and expand our horizons while creating trusting relationships with others. Most importantly, an open environment like this allows us to be proactive and share our input without putting people's personal feelings in jeopardy. However, to have this, we have to learn to distinguish between constructive and destructive criticism, which means distinguishing between fake friends and true friends.

Fake Friends

This can be difficult to accept, but not everyone you know will be delighted to see you doing well. Some will see your success as a threat; others will see it as an implicit criticism of them – if you can do it, why can't they, and if other people have started to see you as the bee's knees, how do they see them? If this is how they're thinking, they'll want to put you down, bringing you back to their level or even below. This is easy enough to deal with if they make their hostility clear – as some will – but others will pretend to be your friend, and they can be a real menace.

I said to Ava, "How many of your friends are like this? I don't know. I once read an article about a scientific study that suggested it could be as many as half of the friends you think you have. I'm not sure what evidence they have to back up their findings, but it does suggest that we should be cautious. The article also stated that most of us aren't good at perceiving the real nature of our friendships and our friends, and this isn't hard to believe. Sadly, even some of the people you think of as good friends don't genuinely want what's best for you. When you think about it for a moment, it doesn't really come as a surprise."

There's nothing better than a true friendship; a reciprocal friendship, but a friendship that you treat as true, only to have others abuse is the worst. What no-one wants is to find they've made a priority of someone who only sees them as an option. It's known that people in reciprocal relationships enjoy greater progress and overall success in life as a result of the influence true friendship brings. Fake friendships are distracting at best and damaging at worst, no matter where you find them.

True friendships are extremely valuable, and they can improve your life in a number of ways. For example, it's said that someone with healthy friends is five times more likely to be healthy themselves. Having true friends that are a positive influence makes you better at what you do, and true friendship makes life more enjoyable in general. In short, true friendship gives life more meaning, but in accepting that there's nothing better than a true friend, you're also accepting that there's nothing worse than a fake friend. Just as a true friend can improve your life in every way, a fake friend can destroy it. Fake friends can pull you off course and make you give up on yourself and your goals. No friend is worth sacrificing your goals for, especially fake friends, so you must eliminate them from your life.

To sum this up for Ava, I said, "Most people know they have fake friends, but never take action to get rid of them because it would make them feel bad. So, this brings us full circle to the discussion about constructive and destructive criticism. The only way to keep making progress in life is to leave negative people behind."

At this point, Ava questioned how she could know who these fake friends are. So to answer this, I said, "It isn't difficult. Fake friends are highly conditional. They are only there for you when it's convenient, when you agree with them, or when you're not pursuing your goals. When you're down and out, your companionship makes a fake friend feel superior, and they might only support you when your plans involve something they've already done themselves or something that suits them. Otherwise, they're inconsistent and unreliable; all talk and no action, paying only lip service to your needs, and offering only circumstantial support and weak encouragement. These people don't care about your goals, and they don't care about you. All they care about are their own goals and, if you're not careful, the result will be that you forget about your own goals and dedicate yourself to theirs instead.

"Fake friends are just in it for themselves and the way you make *them* feel. As soon as you stop making them feel good, they will cut you out. To them, your friendship is highly conditional. If you don't mirror their actions, these fake friends will wreak havoc on your life, potentially belittling you and undermining you in every way possible as they put their efforts into making you miserable. As soon as you start to make changes and begin to make progress, it's the fake friends around you that will pressure you into getting back to where they want you to belong – beneath them."

After thinking about this, Ava quite rightly pointed out that these may be friends you've had for a long time, and questioned what you should do then. I explained that it would make no difference, as history means nothing when it comes to friends. Things change. She was going to grow and change, and they were going to change. The person that was meant to be in her life yesterday may not be meant to be in her life today or tomorrow. Fake friends have a way of holding you captive in your past for the rest of your life, if you let them. They will keep you as the person you have always been. They will keep you from improving or becoming anything else.

Loyalty is not based on history or obligation, but on values and character. I added, "It's important to realise that your job is to go after what you want in this life without being trapped by obligations that limit your freedom and skew your perspective. The only way to gain a better perspective is to create distance. Distance creates clarity. When you are enmeshed in other people's lives, especially the lives of fake friends, you cease to see clearly. The only way to correct your perspective is to physically remove yourself from your current environment. Reduce the clutter of fake friends in your life and you will start seeing clearly again."

I could see that Ava felt uneasy with what I'd just said, asking, "Isn't it a bit hypocritical to keep changing your friend circle as you are growing? Can't I try to bring them along with me?" She was making a good point, because I agree that you should always try to bring about positive change in others – and it will work with some. They're the ones that will join you, or at least support you, but they are your true friends. It's the ones that don't buy into your journey, or those that try to discourage you and hold you back that you need to be aware of. This is not to say that our friendships are going to be sunshine and rainbows at every turn. Good friendships are not always comfortable, and a positive way to view this is to consider that a friendship that doesn't bring challenges is a friendship that's outgrown.

If you're ambitious and motivated in life, you'll outgrow your friendships regularly. This isn't something to feel bad about; it's a good thing, and your focus should be on finding new, like-minded people who have their own goals in life, allowing you to continue pursuing yours alongside them – independently, but in parallel. In effect, you're finding true friendship that revolves around mutual accountability, and these friendships should be stimulating. Cutting someone out of your life doesn't make you a bad person. If you're doing it for the right reasons, it makes you a better person.

Ava's next question showed a great deal of perceptiveness. She said, "But what if I am the fake friend?"

This was a brilliant question. It put me in mind of the old saying about doing to others as you would be done to yourself. Every once in a while, it's a good idea to look at ourselves and the way we behave towards those we regard as friends and ask ourselves if we're being authentic. We should question if the way we're behaving towards our friends is the way we would want them to behave towards us, and give consideration to the possibility that we may be the ones showing some of the signs of being a fake friend.

Question whether you project your own negative qualities onto your friend. Do you assume that because you think or behave a certain way, your friends also think or behave that way? Do you ever talk about others behind their back? And, if you do, do you assume everyone else does the same? Doing so is never good, and it inevitably only ever leads to blaming others for happenings in your life instead of taking personal responsibility. This is something your friends will notice. If you're talking behind someone else's back, they'll be questioning if you're doing the same to them.

If you're criticising other people, or blaming them for everything that's happening to you, you're putting yourself into a place where nothing is ever your fault, and you are always right. This is a place where you lose friends. If you believe that everything is wrong because of them, then you're going to be sending out all sorts of non-verbal messages that let them know what you're thinking, even if you're not saying it out loud.

When Heathrow Airport opened Terminal 4, it was assigned to British Airways. All the advance publicity proudly proclaimed that the terminal was now built around a baggage handling system that would never go wrong again – not something that could ever have been said about the previous BA baggage handling system.

However, the first few days were disastrous, with passengers flying to one destination and their bags going to another. The chief executive of BA announced that he took full responsibility. Having said, "The buck stops here," he then fired the manager responsible for the terminal's operations. This sort of thing happens all too often in business. Saying *I* take responsibility shouldn't be followed up with who is being fired, but it happens, and it makes a joke of the whole thing. Before criticising, you need to make sure you're not making a joke of yourself.

Something else a fake friend will do is only ever call or text when they need something. If this is you, it's going to be noticed by others, and you might find that you're the one being dropped. Real friends take an interest in each other, and listen to what their friends have to say. They don't leap in with their own stories intended to trump their friends' opinions. They realise that true conversation is not simply a matter of allowing someone to speak for a given period of time in return for the right to speak for the same period; they *listen*. To be able to do this, they understand that truly listening to someone is a skill that has to be acquired.

Being able to put yourself in the shoes of someone else demonstrates emotional intelligence. You may find yourself in the position of having something you need to say to someone, but you know it's likely to be hurtful. With emotional intelligence, you consider the other person's feelings, and you find a way to word what you need to say to get the message across without making them feel awful. This may sound like common sense, but common sense isn't always common. In fact, a psychiatrist will tell you that the single thing that really marks out a psychopath is an inability to feel what someone else feels. I'm not suggesting for a moment that a fake friend is a psychopath, but it's fair to say that fake friends will generally not give the feelings of others any consideration at all, and may not even care what effect their words or actions have on others.

At this point I said to Ava, "I know how difficult it can be to listen, because I've often found myself *pretending* to listen, but really I'm just waiting my turn to speak. If everyone listened to each other more, I suspect we'd have fewer wars, fewer divorces, less arguing, better understanding, and more compassion. Something trainee salespeople are told is that a good salesperson has two ears and one mouth – in that proportion. What we all need to realise is that this doesn't only apply to salespeople." Of course, after saying this, I realised that

I'd been doing a lot of talking to get to this point, so I added, "I've been going on and I'm probably become boring, so I'll say just one thing more on this subject: If you want to keep good friendships, stick to your word. If you say you will do something, do it. And be punctual. Don't be the person who is consistently an hour later than promised."

Being a Good Friend

I was pleased when Ava said she didn't think I'd been going on for too long, but she did point out that I'd been talking about what a good friend *wouldn't* do, so she wanted to know now what the opposite of that would be. "If I want to be a good friend to others, what should I do?" she asked.

In my answer, I set out the following:

- **Always be there for her friends.**
  The moment you get the feeling that something is wrong, you should go out of your way to make sure they are okay. Knowing that you care can be the single most important thing to a friend in need.

- **Know when to be serious and when not to be.**
  One of the characteristics that mark out the British is the way they find something to laugh at when things are going wrong. This is a good thing, but it must come from the person in difficulty. Be guided by your friends' feelings. Saying things like, "Hey, it's not that bad," or, "Snap out of it," might be meant well, but it's not helpful – or supportive.

Making light of your own concerns is okay, but not those of another. Just be there, ready to listen and ready to help, even if you think the issue is fairly trivial. What you think isn't what matters; if it isn't trivial in your friend's mind, it isn't trivial.

- Go the extra mile when your friends ask for help.
  When a friend asks for your opinion or help with something that matters to them, it means they value what you think. If your friend hands you her essay, asking for your help to proofread or revise it, then go the extra mile. Show them that you are as invested as they are. Commit fully. These are your true friends. It's a committed relationship, and it sucks when the other person doesn't put in any effort to help when needed.

- **Never give up on your friends during their darkest hours.**
  Let them know that you have their back. Remind them that you are a true friend by making sure they know you'll always be there. This means keeping in touch or being there to cheer them up when they are down. It's also important, though, to understand and respect boundaries. Know that you don't need to be together 24/7. You need your own space to recharge, and you won't always feel like hanging out with others, but this doesn't mean you don't like them. Good friends aren't pushy, and they don't get upset by an occasional no. In fact, good friends know how to pick up right where they left off, no matter how long it's been since they last saw each other.

- **Find a way to voice concerns.**
  Consider your friend's feelings before you speak, but be aware that there's a difference between being conscious of their feelings and letting them ruin themselves. If they have developed a bad habit, find a way to mention it and show that you're concerned.

- **Be dependable and learn to apologise.**
  It takes a lot of courage to admit you did something wrong, but don't be afraid to admit that you messed up. It happens to the best of us, and someone that can swallow their pride and admit they're in the wrong is a great friend.

- **And be and stay authentically you.**
  Perhaps most important of all, always be yourself and stay authentic in all you do. Earning the respect of your friends happens by being true to yourself and what you stand for. Your friends will realise that you are a person with value and integrity.

At the end of all that, I smiled and asked, "There. Is that enough practical 'to do' advice?"

I didn't get a direct reply – just, "I think it's time for coffee."

Lasting Friendships

Having talked a lot about friendships, it's probably a good idea to recap on the fact that friendships don't necessarily last. We know this to be true, because talking to those now in their 60s, 70s, 80s or more, confirms it.

Very few friendships last forever. Nevertheless, a friendship that lasts a decade is worth having, so it's worth looking at what makes that happen. A good friendship is built on the foundation of common values. This means your friends share your spiritual, moral, and ethical beliefs. Sharing similar traits and interests can also be important, but be cautious of friendships built on similar interests alone. In simply being a likeable person, you'll effortlessly attract many potential new friendships, and this is because likeable people build up other people's egos.

Everyone has an inbuilt desire to feel important. If I deflate your ego, and therefore your feelings of importance, you may laugh it off, but I have deeply wounded and offended you. I have shown you disrespect, and that's not going to make you like me. But, if I elevate your self-respect and contribute to your feeling of personal worth, I'm showing high esteem for your ego. I've helped you to be your best self and therefore you appreciate what I've done. You are grateful to me, and you like me for it.

End of Day Four

Late in the afternoon, we arrived at Mývatn, a shallow lake in an area of active volcanos in the north of Iceland, not far from Krafla volcano. The lake and the surrounding wetlands provide a habitat for a number of waterbirds, especially ducks. The lake was created by a large basaltic lava eruption 2300 years ago, and the surrounding landscape is dominated by volcanic landforms, including lava pillars and rootless vents. The effluent river Laxá is known for its rich fishing for brown trout and Atlantic salmon. The word Mývatn stands for Midge Lake, and this comes from the large numbers of midges present in the summer. Luckily for us it's December. The River Laxá, Lake Mývatn and the surrounding wetlands are protected as a nature reserve.

We reached our cabin at around six, when it had already been dark for hours. The cabin was small, but in a great, secluded location, and we were happy. We were also very lucky. One of our reasons for staying here was that we hoped to see the Northern Lights – and we did! What an amazing sight.

Chapter 6
Let the World Be Your Playground

"The world is a book and those who do not travel read only a page."
– Saint Augustine

Day 5: Godafoss, Akureyri, Hvammstangi

We began the morning driving to Godafoss, which translates as Waterfall of the Gods. This was right off the Ring Road and very easy to access, and although not as tall as the other waterfalls we'd visited, it has a beautifully unique horseshoe shape. Our next stop was to fill up on petrol and stock up on groceries after grabbing some lunch in Akureyri, the second largest urban area in Iceland. With a population of 18,000 and nicknamed "Capital of the North", Akureyri is an old trading station and an important port and fishing centre.

The area was settled in the 9th century, but it didn't receive a municipal charter until 1786. Allied units were based in the town during World War II, and further growth occurred after the war as the Icelandic population increasingly moved to urban areas. Geographical factors give the area a relatively mild climate and the town's ice-free harbour has played a significant role in its history. We enjoyed our short time there and hope to be back soon to spend more time exploring it.

The Love for Travel

Ava said, "I can really see why you love Iceland so much. It's a truly beautiful place."

It has always been my general philosophy on travel to never to go to the same place twice because there are so many amazing places to explore, but Iceland has proved to be the exception. My love for travel is so evident that it came as a surprise to Ava that I was 19 before I boarded an aircraft. With South Africa in isolation during the apartheid years, opportunities to travel aboard were limited, but once I did, I was hooked.

For me, there is no better feeling than stepping onto foreign soil for the first time. You could say I measure every expense in terms of flight tickets. If I see a jacket I want to buy, a voice inside me reminds me that I could get a flight to Europe or beyond for the price of it. The same curiousness to explore is something we've wanted to instill in Ava from a very young age. We took her everywhere with us: when she was nine months old, we hiked up Prykestollen in Norway, with her on my back. I remember people looked at us oddly, but she was smiling from ear to ear. It made me want her to continue experiencing interesting places as she became older. We might live in an apartment in Buckinghamshire, but I always wanted the world to be Ava's playground, and for her to experience the beauty of our amazing planet and all it can teach us.

I can't remember a time when I wasn't dreaming about exploring a faraway place. Travelling is always front of mind for me. Our calendar is usually fully booked at least a year in advance, and sometimes longer. My vision board in the kitchen is full of places still to visit, and I love this because we're always looking forward. It's not unusual for people to adopt an attitude of "all good things come to an end", but this is not the case for us as when one trip ends, we start looking forward to the next. It makes me wonder where this thinking comes from; why should good things ever end?

Trying to answer why I love travel is like trying to answer why I love to eat condensed milk. I just do. I know condensed milk isn't to everyone's taste (in fact, I know a family where it's always referred to as condemned milk), but I love it, and that's that. Others may find the yearning for travel more understandable, though even that has its limits for some. The poet Philip Larkin, a noted stay-at-home, was once asked if he'd like to see China. He replied that he wouldn't mind going to China, as long as he could get home the same day. He was notoriously down in the mouth about many things, but for me, there's something magical about getting the chance to spend time in a new place, surrounded by new sights, and experiencing new food, people, and cultures.

I think exposure to these new experiences can be personally reviving, and seeing how other people live can be a real eye-opener. We all have biases and preconceptions. They surround us from our earliest days in the form of the things our parents, friends, and teachers think, and they become what we think. On a global scale, these thoughts are sometimes right and sometimes wrong. Some of the preconceived ideas we hold are harmless, but some can do real damage. The quickest way to question our preconceptions is to go to a different country and get first-hand knowledge for ourselves.

Travel can be a humbling experience. It's easy to have your status quo at home, but as soon as you're in a new place, you need to adapt. This can be both scary and rewarding. It can be sobering to realise that the life you live is not the only one you could live. It can be a source of freedom to understand that in the grand scheme of things, the worries that consume you are pretty insignificant. We can get so caught up in our daily lives that we forget just how easy we have it. The only limits we have are the ones we create for ourselves, and travelling helps make sure we don't forget that.

Another great benefit of travel is that it takes you out of your comfort zone. Challenge leads to curiosity, maturity, and growth. You automatically become a more curious being, not least because when you travel, the most basic things such as catching a bus between cities can become an adventure, and you are instantly more aware of your surroundings. Greater awareness allows you to appreciate the beauty or intrigue of a new land and culture, and when you return home, you also see your familiar environment in a whole new light.

Having future trips already planned brings me joy and gives me something to look forward to, so in this sense it's an escape from daily stress. I've never regretted a single trip I've taken. We get so involved in our own life and environment that the chance to step out, explore, and experience elsewhere gives us perspective, often providing new lenses through which to see and think about who we are, what we are doing with our lives, and what we care about. The whole experience is filled with all these beautiful and crazy colours and feelings.

I said to Ava, "Whenever I was travelling, I always told your grandparents that I was on a journey to find myself. When I got back at the end of the trip, they'd always ask if I'd achieved it – had I found myself. Of course, what I didn't know then but know now is that life is not about finding yourself, it's about the journey; a journey where you never arrive because you're relentlessly on a quest to achieve higher standards, new experiences, and continued growth. Every travel experience is a new adventure, and a new journey of discovery and learning. Discovering new things is an amazing feeling..."

It was at this point, having gone on at some length, that Ava wanted to challenge my point. She said, "But do you really need to travel to experience new things in life?" And, of course, you don't. You're at home, you walk out of your front door, turn left or right, or go straight ahead, and within 100 metres there'll be something you haven't seen before, something you don't know about, *if* you have your eyes and ears open. So, no, travel is not the only way to explore new things, but it's the one I find most satisfactory, and I think that's because when you travel, ignoring the new is not possible. When you're at home, it's not only possible, but likely. When you travel, you get away from daily routine and daily chores. It's a break from your everyday reality and a chance to see what everyday reality is for others. However, something else that can't be ignored is the change to travel that *9/11* and the Coronavirus pandemic has brought. Travel now involves all kinds of security measures and regulations that weren't there before, so it's fair to say that the free-spirited aspect I once knew has all but disappeared.

Time to Reflect

An often-overlooked aspect of travel is the benefit of being lost. The thought of getting lost being a good thing made Ava laugh, but when you think about it, life at home is usually so planned and structured that getting "lost" in an adventure is good for the soul. When you're lost, you need to pay close attention to everything around you to help you figure out what you should say or do in an unfamiliar situation. In terms of a different culture, this might be knowing how to be respectful, and it's through being "lost" that you begin to question and reflect on your own assumptions and behaviour.

Through travel, you are effectively representing your home nation, and this puts you in a position to consider other people's perspectives. Knowing that other people also have preconceived ideas can make the way you behave and present yourself worthy of extra thought. When I first started travelling, I'd wear my Springbok rugby jersey everywhere I went. That jersey served as a magnet, attracting conversations about rugby, not only with other South Africans, but in other rugby-loving nations such as Fiji, Tonga, and even Tahiti.

There's nothing quite like getting off a plane/train/bus and seeing the beauty of a new place for the first time. There can be times when the outer beauty is so overwhelming that I need to stand still and let time stop, to try to take it all in at once. This was certainly the case when I got my first glimpse of the Grand Canyon. Until that day, I'd never known that the experience of something can literally take your breath away. The beauty of the place is so astonishing that I had to gasp for air. Sometimes, the beauty of a place is less about aesthetics and more about the first conversation with a local; those moments when I'm pleasantly overwhelmed by their openness and rich culture. I love to walk several miles each day in a new place and think about who has walked there before me. It can be startling to realise that I don't know a single person for miles and miles, but I think that's part of the excitement.

I feel most alive when I'm exploring. There's a floor tile in an airport in Norway that really resonated with me. On it, it states that every step and decision you have taken in your whole life has led you to stand right there on that tile. When I first read it, it made me realise that you can only stand somewhere else for the first time by trying to get there. There was another floor marking that really gave me an insight into the country I was visiting. I had landed at Auckland airport in New Zealand and needed to get straight onto a domestic flight. I asked a local for directions to the domestic terminal, and he said, "Go through that door. You'll see a blue line on the floor. Follow it, and you'll find the domestic terminal at the other end." He then added, "We put it there so Australians don't get lost." That comment contained a wealth of information about the relationship between the two closely-linked countries, as did the comment made by the purser of the Qantas flight landing in Auckland from Melbourne: "Welcome to New Zealand. Please turn your watch back 50 years."

Travel may be considered an escape from worries, but in reality, worries will always follow you. However, travel does give you an opportunity to put them in perspective.

In my late 20s, my girlfriend and I had just broken up; I decided that the cure was a solo travel adventure around the world. During that trip I went to Cambodia and India, and it was such an eye-opener. They are both beautiful countries with amazing people, but the poverty in some areas was a shock to the system. I'd known about it in theory, of course, but knowing something with your head and knowing it in your heart are two different things. It made me realise how trivial my worries were and how fortunate I really was.

One of the great advantages of living in the UK is the easy access it provides to interesting people, beautiful landscapes, incredible food, amazing music, and different cultures, all within a short distance of home. In one day, you can sip wine in France, eat pasta in Italy, and then nibble chocolates in Switzerland for dessert. All this is on the UK's doorstep, and yet there are people you meet who've never left the country. In some cases, they've never left their home county, and I once met an old lady who'd never left her hometown of Gillingham. I'm not judging anyone who chooses not to travel, but I know a life of no travel wouldn't do for me.

Moving away from the well-worn tourist trails whenever possible will provide the greatest benefits. Explore where the locals eat, drink, dance, and live. In Cyprus, for example, places like Paphos have pizzerias, Irish bars, and burger joints one after the other, so other than having sunny weather, this makes them just like Dartford, Blackpool, or Slough. They're also full of British people, so it begs the question of why people travel only to experience what they already have at home? Perhaps sunshine is all that matters, but Cyprus has so much more to explore and discover, not least the wonderful restaurants serving Greek meze.

I heard a similar story from someone who'd been on a cycling holiday in Burgundy – the kind where you cycle on your own, but a company moves your luggage onto the next place every second day. On his first evening in Auxerre, he found his way to a restaurant overlooking the river and ate *boeuf bourguignon* (which he said was delicious). The following morning, another English couple on the same trip asked if he'd enjoyed his meal. They asked because they'd opted to eat pizza – something familiar. There they were in Burgundy, the home of *boeuf bourguignon*, *coq au vin*, and a host of other wonderful dishes, yet they'd eaten pizza. Why? Why go there and eat a meal they could have had by staying at home in Blackpool. It's a question that's hard to answer, and I simply don't understand how people can have the opportunity to try something different and not take it. Not judging, just stating...

Even frustrating travel experiences can end up being some of the most memorable, and some of the most hilarious stories to share and reminisce over. I remember a trip to Kenya that made me examine and question how I live and what's important to me. I see such discrepancies between my life and others, and the trip left me wondering who's really happier. Although we live in a nice apartment with all the trappings and material things we can desire, the people I saw in the villages had broader smiles. The kids were running around barefoot, and no-one there was experiencing any of the frustrations we inflict on ourselves with concerns over slow broadband or no signal on our mobile phones. It made me think to myself about which life is better. This existential question is brought into sharper focus for me by travelling to countries where the cultures, customs, and socioeconomic levels are different to those I grew up with.

Why Travel?

This topic led Ava and I into a conversation about how often one should travel – not just go on holiday, as we were in Iceland. Going on holiday and serious travel are two different things. To travel, you need to take your time, not plan everything to the last detail as we had, but leave some things (perhaps even a lot) to chance, effectively seeing where the next road might take you without knowing. To really travel, your life needs to be set up in a way that allows you to pack your bags for a few weeks or months and just go.

There's no better feeling for me than putting my rucksack on my back, taking my passport in my hand, and heading to the airport. But let's be honest, young adults and retired people are going to find serious travel easier to fit into their lifestyle than most others. The reason is simple: completely carefree travel once you have a partner and children is a lot more difficult. It can be done – people do it – but it requires an awful lot of planning, and the number of things that can go wrong is greater. It also demands that everyone involved has the same objectives; I can't think of anything more disastrous than one partner wanting to spend a couple of years moving slowly around Southeast Asia while the other is worried about career opportunities slipping away, for example.

My advice to Ava was to travel as much, as far, and as often as she can before settling into a life of careers, mortgages, marriage, and children. There are 195 countries (currently) in the world, so why not make it a goal to see them all? I said, "Wouldn't that be great? Take a year or more after school and go see the world. Go figure out what it is that you want to do and study for. Don't be like me when I went to Uni. I didn't know until the morning of registration what I was going to study. I left it all so late. My parents took me to a school in Johannesburg. I knew I wanted to study business, so I got a list of degree courses on offer, picked one, went for an interview, and that`s what I studied for the next four years. If I'd taken the opportunity to spend some time exploring the world first and immersing myself in it, I would have come back clearer in my mind about what I wanted to know, and therefore what I wanted to study.

"Don`t make the mistake I made. Make your 20s a time to explore. Work somewhere for a year, take a few months off, work again somewhere else, and then travel again for a year or so. I made the mistake lots of people make in their late teens and early 20s – I took life too seriously. You're surrounded by people – parents, teachers, uncles, and aunts – who tell you that if you don't get on board the gravy train right now, it will leave the station and you'll never catch up with it. I know now that this is nonsense. If I had my time again, I'd wait until my 30s before getting seriously focused on a career."

I also pointed out that we need to be aware of how much life is changing. Just by looking back at companies in Britain 60 years ago, the differences are many. There were far fewer service industry companies back then, and far more people than today were involved in manufacturing, mining, and transport. Many of the jobs that existed in the 1950s no longer exist. In manufacturing, there'd be enormous rooms full of draughtsmen, almost all male, standing at drawing boards and drawing the parts that would be manufactured to make a product.

There'd be other departments employing people (most of them female) at accounting machines, producing invoices, dispatch notes, purchase orders, and all the other documentation a manufacturing company needed. Back then, you wouldn't find managers writing their own letters on their own laptops, as they do now. There were personal assistants, secretaries, and shorthand typists who'd sit across from the manager at his desk and take down what he said in shorthand, then use a typewriter to turn it into a letter or some other document. Most of the people in these jobs were female, and most of the people operating the tools and machines, or fixing the machines, were male.

Almost all of those jobs are now gone because of computers, but this doesn't mean we have huge numbers of people out of work. The jobs that disappeared were replaced by other jobs, and almost all of those new jobs were more interesting and more satisfying than the jobs that had gone. These changes came about largely in the late 1960s and all through the 1970s, but change is still happening. Thanks to laptops and ever-changing technology, an increasing number of people no longer need to go into an office building to work. Some jobs can be done from anywhere. My advice to Ava was to take advantage of that, and focus on the kind of creative work that would allow her to work from any location and on her own clock, provided the work is done. Working for yourself in the growing field of eCommerce is an option, and it's an option that allows travelling to be a part of life – you can run an on-line shop while you're sitting on a beach in Bali.

Travel changes you, and it's up to each of us to decide what form the changes will take. When I moved to England, I was an Afrikaans boy from a small town, and people told me how quiet I was. Actually, I don't think I was quiet; I appeared that way because I had to translate what I wanted to say in my mind from Afrikaans to English before I could say it out loud. This all took time, so I often opted not to say anything. It meant I had two personalities: my normal self when I was around people in my comfort zone, and the more introverted version of me I became around my new English friends. But I persevered, and my confidence soon grew as I came to realise that I could do things despite the obstacles I faced. In fact, through perseverance, those obstacles soon become much less obstructive and more like welcome challenges. The move from South Africa also helped me develop cultural sensitivity. Growing up in apartheid South Africa, there were always tensions between cultures. South Africa is culturally very diverse, and while that should really be seen as a strength and something to be proud of as a nation, other cultures within the country were seen as something to be protected against. How silly is that? To learn the values and uniqueness of different cultures is one of the most rewarding things you can ever experience.

I said to Ava, "Being culturally sensitive is key in our globalising world. It's not enough to say, 'People from X country are like this,' it's important to look for underlying values that may explain a certain behaviour in order to practise cultural sensitivity. A good example of this was when I was in Spain. In the south of the country, they take a two or three-hour lunch and siesta in the middle of their workday. Many other cultures might view this as the people just being lazy, but in fact, it's historically about Spaniards valuing family face time. Eating together as a family is more important to them than maximising work time by scoffing a quick sandwich at their work desks.

"Being aware of other cultural values and norms can help us better understand international issues and conflicts. It makes you realise how small the world really is and that at its heart almost all people are good people with the same dreams and anxieties as you. It makes you realise that rather than building higher walls, we should be building bigger tables. I also believe that later in your career, having a world view will make you a more balanced person and give you a competitive edge. Use the confidence and cultural sensitivity that traveling helps you develop to make you successful."

Travel also provides an opportunity to become immersed in a second or even a third language. Something we take for granted in England, and something that would appear to be an unspoken expectation, is that all other nations should speak English. It's an expectation that makes us lazy when it comes to learning a new language. Once you travel abroad, especially around Europe, you realise that almost everyone you meet speaks at least two languages with some degree of proficiency. Being able to speak another language means that you can order meals and arrange transport and accommodation in the country that language belongs to, but it also gives you something else. When you learn how German people structure their words and sentences, for example, you are also learning another way of thinking.

In the business world, speaking another language and understanding another culture can be the difference that makes the difference in any negotiation. An international salesman I knew once told me of an experience he had in France. He was doing business in France, but he had never let it be known that he spoke French. What he discovered was that the French businessmen were saying one thing to him in English and then quite another thing among themselves in French. He told me, "I'm also fluent in German, which was known, and I never had those problems doing business in Germany. Make of that what you will."

Finally, and perhaps most importantly, if you don't speak other languages, you may never learn what a friendly place this world can be. Most people, wherever they are, want to be friendly. If you can't communicate with them, you've made it harder.

End of Day Five

Our final destination of the day was Hvammstangi, a village in the north-west of the country. It's the most densely populated area in the Húnaþing County, with a population of about 580 people.

Hvammstangi is also an important service centre for the surrounding area. It's a regional provider of education, and it has been an important trading centre since 1846. The village has a growing tourism industry, and fishing is very important to its economy, but it's also home to the largest textile factory in Iceland.

We were told that Hvammstangi is known for its seals, but even after taking a drive near the shore, we didn't manage to see any. The Seal Centre in the village went some way towards lifting our disappointment, but at around 10 in the evening, the sight we saw from our cabin window made up for everything – the Northern Lights. This time they were even brighter and more actively dancing around than anything we'd seen before, and we felt incredibly lucky to be seeing them again.

Chapter 7
The Platinum Rule

"God grant me the serenity to accept the things I cannot change, the courage to change the things I can, and the wisdom to know the difference." – Reinhold Niebuhr

Day 6: Hólmavík, Ísafjörður, and Stykkisholmur

We ventured a little into the fjords to see what there was to see. We drove up to Holmavik, a village in the western part of Iceland, the largest settlement in Strandir, and a centre of commerce for the county. Hólmavík is part of the Strandabyggð municipality and has 375 inhabitants. It's also home to the Museum of Icelandic Sorcery and Witchcraft – a place we decided we could live without seeing – and it boasts a swimming pool constructed in 2004. Why is this interesting? Because it's the only pool in the region not geothermally heated. It still amazes me every time how energy efficient Iceland is.

To get even more stunning views, we drove a couple of hours to Ísafjörður, a town in the northwest of Iceland. The name means fjord of ice, and with a population of about 2,600, it's the largest settlement in the West Fjords.

In the Beginning

The beauty of these mountains and the ocean brought on a conversation about exactly where it all comes from. I suggested that being in a place like this gave an appreciation of God's goodness, and Ava agreed because she has been brought up with a Christian belief. "But," she said, "in school we're taught about Darwin's theory of evolution and that everything was created by chance and not by God. We were asked at the end of the lesson what we thought of it, and I couldn't speak up about the creation. I know that we believe God created everything, but how can I explain that in simple terms?"

It's one of the hardest things we have to deal with, and we have to accept that people will disagree with us all through our life – but rarely with such vigour as they will about belief. I said, "Believing in God is unfortunately not the modern and popular way for most people today, but we shouldn't let that worry us. As someone I know once said, 'When everyone knows something, the one thing you can be sure of is that the something everyone knows is wrong.' I think that's a good rule to live by. If you find that the majority agrees with you, you should start worrying.

"Matthew said it best for me when he told us of the need to enter through the narrow gate, '...for wide is the gate and broad is the road that leads to destruction, and many enter through it. But small is the gate and narrow the road that leads to life, and only few find it.' This is a particularly useful lesson today when the most ludicrous nonsense gets bandied around on social media and everyone comes to believe it. People are so gullible."

It isn't easy at times to stick to what you believe. I remember being one of only five boys in school in

South Africa who refused to do military drills due to our religious beliefs. The five of us had to stand in front of the whole school while they practised war drills. At 16 it takes some guts to stand up for your belief. I could have easily just done the drills, and no-one would have known any better, but I had strong faith in what I believed was right. I just could not accept that a loving God would want me to learn how to kill on command from any political leader. I was never able to accept the contradiction that when you kill on the instructions of your country's leader, you are a hero, but when you kill outside of that, you are a murderer. Killing is killing.

The same goes for the debate between creation and evolution. Nature, for me, is just too perfect to be by accident or chance. People will say that it's not by chance and took billions of years for us to get to this point, but I still cannot accept that theory. It makes me think of all the components that make up a computer: if you place all the thousands of components in a tumble drier and let it spin – can I believe that eventually, billions of years from now, all the components would perfectly join each other in order to have a working computer? My simple mind can't comprehend that's possible.

I said to Ava, "When someone tells you in all seriousness that we now understand the universe, how it came into being, and how it works, you must accept that they believe what they're saying, but you must also remember that they don't *really* know. We don't understand how the universe came into being and we don't know how it works. There are theories, and some of the theories have a ring of truth about them, but they are still only partial. And if you talk to a physicist exploring the origins of the universe, they'll soon start answering questions with, 'We don't know the answer to that, and we may never know it. We have some theories, but that's what they are – theories.'

"When I hear people attempting to answer the questions about what came before the Big Bang and what caused it, I can't help but be reminded of the story about science having progressed to the point where it's just possible to make out a sound made a moment before the Big Bang happened. At that distance in time, it's naturally difficult to make out exactly what the sound is, but there's general agreement that it sounds very like, 'Oops'. What I don't understand is why choosing to believe that there was an intelligent design behind the creation of the universe, and that someone or something (which I choose to call God) was behind that design, causes so many people to get furious."

I once asked a chiropractor how chiropractic works. He replied by saying, "I don't know. And nor do I know, though I accept other people do, what happens to make the light come on when I press a switch, but I know it does." That's how I feel about the universe: I don't understand it, I don't know where it came from or how it works, but I know it does. Scientists have told us, and I believe them, that life on earth is only possible because of an almost unimaginable combination of factors like distance from the sun, size of the planet, nature of the atmosphere, a particular balance of elements in the rocks that formed earth, and a number of other things. Some people will say that this amazing combination of coincidences proves that God does not exist. To me, it proves the opposite.

To answer Ava's original question about persuading non-believers, I put forward another question, "Why would you want to? They have their beliefs, which I take it they are happy with, so why interfere with them? The only thing I would add to that is that the best way to show your faith to another is in the way you act. Your behaviour, your readiness, or otherwise, to forgive people, is likely to be far more persuasive than any words you can string together."

The Platinum Rule

The golden rule instructs that we should treat other people the way we would want them to treat us. It's a very good rule, but there's also something we can think of as the platinum rule. It comes from the New Testament and it's very simple. Matthew's gospel says that when Jesus was asked what the most important law God had given was, he said, "Love the Lord your God with all your heart and with all your soul and with all your mind." He then went on to say that there was a second law, "Love your neighbour as yourself." So, there it is: "You shall love the Lord your God with all your heart and with all your soul and you shall love your neighbour as yourself." We can argue that that's all there is, and Jesus did exactly that when he said, "All the Law and the Prophets hang on these two commandments." This is why I call this the platinum rule, and we should keep it in our minds at all times.

ASPIRE FOR ABUNDANCE

Over the last two thousand and some years, the Christian religion has come to be hung about with all sorts of things that, if you read the Bible, simply aren't there. People were told that they could buy indulgences; by giving money to the church they could shorten the time their dead loved ones spent in Purgatory. There's no mention of any of this in the Bible, not even the idea of Purgatory. There are so many other examples of this, but what it comes down to is that religion (and I don't mean just the Christian religion) has been picked up by rulers and governments as a way of keeping their people in order. All sorts of things have been added, and if you ask what authority there is for them, the answer will usually be that there is none. Almost everything you learn at Sunday school and in church can be dispensed with, when you come right down to it, but what cannot be got rid of is that simple instruction: love God with all your heart and with all your soul, and love your neighbour as yourself, meaning treat others as you would want others to treat you.

I said to Ava, "Think of the Bible as an owner's manual for anyone with a life. You wouldn't try to set up a smart TV without reading the instructions, and yet many people dive straight into their life without thinking about what they're doing. Life is a lot more complicated than any TV yet made. The people who make the TV supply a manual, so did the being who created us. Read it. Ideally, not just when the thought enters your mind, but every day. Think about what it says. Philippians tells us not to be anxious over anything. We all do better when we become aware of our spirituality and how every living thing is connected to Infinite Intelligence.

The universe and God want you to live an abundant life, nature only knows abundance, but in order to have that life, you must first seek God's loving wisdom so that everything else will be given to you. That is my most important guideline for you, Ava. Love Jehovah with all your heart and I can promise you that no problem will ever be too big for you to handle."

God Wants You to Do Well

Something to remember when you're talking to bright teens is that they don't forget what you said. Ava reminded me, "Dad, you said we shouldn't pursue riches but rather pursue building our faith with God. Does that mean that we can't work to have nice things? Does it mean we need to be poor?"

This echoed what I used to ask myself when I was growing up. There was a time when I believed there was no relationship between faith and prosperity, that when one speaks about religion one should never relate it to achievement; that it dealt only with ethics and morals or social values. But I was wrong. An idea like that limits God's power, and nothing so limiting is going to make sense in the end. There's a tremendous power in the universe and this power can dwell in each one of us. It is a power that can blast out all defeat and lift a person above all difficult situations. By the full and proper use of your individual power, stimulated by God's power, you can make your life successful.

I said to Ava, "Religion brought me lifesaving spiritual values. It gave me a new zest for life. It gave me faith, hope, and courage. It banished tensions, anxieties, fears, and worries. It gave purpose and direction to my life. Faith in God vastly improved my happiness. I can say with complete confidence that if you put 100% faith in God, your future will be bright. Do you need to be poor to be in God's favour? You don't, but let's be clear on this: self-worth and net worth are two different things. Your value is not determined by your valuables. God says that the most valuable things in life are not 'things'. The most common myth about money is that having more will make you more secure. It will not. I know from experience that money can be lost through a variety of uncontrollable factors, and I also know that real security can only be found in that which can never be taken from you – your relationship with God.

"However, I do believe strongly that God did not create us to struggle. For us to not struggle, we need money, and quite a lot of it if we are going to enjoy everything God created for us to enjoy. Many people genuinely believe that material success is a sin or that it's not intended for them. I don't believe that for one second. God blessed many of His loyal servants with great riches. Think of Job, Abraham, and Solomon. Think of the whole nation of Israel being led to the land of milk and honey. The story of Paradise being given to Adam and Eve tells you that abundance is desirable and intended. A fully alive human being is the glory of God, and to be fully alive, in this system of things, we need money. I think if we see money simply as a means to an end or as a tool to live the life we want, then all is fine. To pursue money for the sake of just having more money and not use it as a tool for an enriched life for you and others is not what God wants for us."

This seemed to make sense to Ava, and she ended the conversation by saying, "The purpose of life, then, is not to seek riches but to seek God's approval?"

The Purpose of Life

I agree with Ava's summation. Without a purpose, life is motion without meaning, activity without direction, and events without reason. Without a purpose, life is trivial, petty, and pointless. I believe that purpose-driven living leads to a simpler lifestyle. Knowing your purpose focusses your life. You become effective by being selective. Knowing your purpose also energises your life. Purpose always produces passion. Nothing motivates like a clear purpose.

Of course, this still leaves the question of what that purpose should be. For me, the answer is clear: our first purpose in life should be to worship God. That is our number one responsibility – the platinum rule. Some people have missed the most important thing in life; they do not know God. You may know a lot about a lot of things, but if you don't know God personally, you're missing the purpose of life. To worship God is more than just going to meetings on Sundays. Worshipping God is a lifestyle. The Bible says, "By your fruits you will be known to be my followers," with fruits meaning how you behave.

Then, I'd say the second purpose of your life should be to love your neighbour as yourself – the golden rule.

Jesus said that as he loves us, so we must love another, and he also said, "All men will know that you are my disciples if you have love for one another." This is such a far-reaching and important rule. This one rule encompasses so many. If you love your fellow man as though he were you, you will not steal from him, you will not hurt him, you will not say bad things about him. This can be easier said than done, as revenge for perceived wrongs is a deep-seated human driver, but all we can do is be aware of this golden rule and keep striving for it, however imperfect we may be.

This brings me to the third purpose of life, and that is to build a Christ-like character. Someone once told me that we should try to live such wholesome lives that if there were ever a breaking news bulletin stating that Jesus was back on earth, people would come up to us and ask if we are Him. This is obviously an impossibility because none of us has that level of perfection, but the point still resonated with me as being a standard we should aspire to. God wants us to grow to spiritual maturity, and spiritual maturity is becoming like Jesus in the way we think, feel, and act. The Bible calls it a new personality.

And so we come to the fourth purpose in life: to tell others about God. To share God's great purpose for people is a great privilege. It's introducing others to the truth, helping them discover their purpose, and this is a challenge as fewer and fewer people are interested in the good news about God and His kingdom. But that doesn't mean we should stop trying. Imagine the fulfilment of knowing that you helped just one person to gain the privileges you experience, and will experience, knowing God. Don't be disheartened when people call you old-fashioned and say that you believe in fairy tales, and that the Bible was written 2000 years ago and is no longer applicable today. Instead, feel energised to find that one person who will be longing to learn more about the blessings that knowing God brings. I always say that I would much rather believe and be proved wrong than not believe and be proved wrong when the end comes.

There are, of course, many other things that add to your purpose in life, including love and support for your family, longevity through healthy living, etc., but life has ultimately no purpose without God. And without purpose, life has no meaning. Without meaning, life has no significance or hope. There's a famous quote by Dr Myles Munroe: "The greatest tragedy is not death but life without purpose."

Eternity

After the death of a well-known person, there's often talk of the legacy they've left. When I hear someone say this, I feel happy that the person who has died has someone who remembers them well, but living to create an earthly legacy is a short-sighted goal. A wiser use of time is to build an eternal legacy. We need to realise that this life is not all there is. We should see our current life on earth as just a dress-rehearsal before the real production. Our time on earth is the staging area.

Searching for a way that Ava could relate to this, I said, "Think of it as a bit like preschool. A try-out for life in eternity. This life is preparation for the next. Just as the nine months you spent in your mother's womb were not an end but a preparation for life, so this life is preparation for the next. Perhaps you may live to be 100 years old. Whoever is on the throne at that time will send you a telegram. People will throw a big party, though you will have to accept that all the guests are younger than you because everyone you grew up with is dead. Your local newspaper will send a reporter, who will want to know your secret for a long life. Their report will list your children, grandchildren, great-grandchildren, and (quite possibly) great-great-grandchildren. You will get all this attention because living for 100 years is a remarkable thing, but it pales into insignificance when you place it beside a life in eternity. Eternal life will be for ever."

I went on to explain that at 14, it may not seem that our lives on earth are short, but the longer you live, the clearer this fact becomes. As you get older, the weeks, months, and years fly by. Once we know this, we realise that there is no time to waste. You can't decide to live a godly life once you've done this or that; the time to start is now. Now is the time to live a life dedicated to God in order to live in paradise forever. I asked Ava if she could remember the popular experiment that was done with kids – they were given the option of having one marshmallow now, or having two later, if they waited. So many kids take the first option and grab the one marshmallow. It's an experiment that demonstrates many of us would rather seek instant gratification than wait for the bigger reward. But it's the bigger reward that accounts for most.

At this point, Ava pointed out that the idea of eternity and forever is one that's hard to get her head around. I agreed, saying, "I know. We learn at quite an early age that we will die one day, but for a very long time it remains the kind of knowledge you have in your head, but not in your heart. We know it, but we don't really *know* it. I don't believe we're meant to live with that knowledge always before us. The Bible says that God planted eternity into our hearts."

I believe that each of us has an inborn instinct that longs for immortality, and we have it because God created us in His image, to live for eternity. Even though we know everyone eventually dies, death always seems unnatural and unfair. The reason we feel we should live forever is that God wired our brains with that desire. We go for specialist treatment when we have a life-threatening illness. We put our seat belts on when driving a car. We do these things because we don't want to die. So many people have said on their deathbeds that they would give up everything just to spend one more day with loved ones. The reason for this is that we will do anything to live. Even though Stoics or others will say that we should accept death, and that death is part of the natural cycle of life, when it really is our time (whether prematurely or after a long life) we want to live.

It's fair to say that many of us turn to God in desperation when we're in despair or at the limit of our own strength. This is summed up by those that say there are no atheists in foxholes, meaning that everyone turns to God in a life-or-death situation. Why is this? Why wait until we're desperate? Why not renew our strength every day? Even though it's true that we will probably die before God restores paradise on earth, we have no reason to fear death if we have a relationship with God. Those that don't have this relationship fear death because it means the end, but those that do know that they are just in the waiting room, and the next destination is paradise.

When you fully comprehend that there's more to life than just the here and now, and you realise that life on earth is just preparation for eternal life in paradise, you will begin to live each day differently. Suddenly, many activities, goals, and even problems that seemed so important will appear trivial, petty, and unworthy of your attention. The closer you live to God, the smaller everything else appears. I said to Ava, "I'm sure we'll not be in paradise for two seconds before we start to wonder why we placed so much importance on things that were so temporary. We'll want to know what we could have been thinking, and why we wasted so much time, energy, and concern on what was not going to last."

When you live with eternity in mind, your values change. You use your time and money wisely. You place a higher premium on relationships and character instead of fame and wealth, achievement, or even fun. The apostle Paul once said that he had at one time thought all these things were so very important, but he then considered them worthless because of what Christ has done for us.

End of Day Six

We arrived in Stykkishólmur late in the afternoon. Stykkishólmur exists because of its natural harbour.

The location became an important trading post early in Iceland's history: the first trading post in Stykkishólmur can be traced back to the mid-16th century, even before Denmark implemented the Danish-Icelandic Trade Monopoly. From that time, trading has been at the heart of the settlement's history.

We had thought our cabin in Hvammstangi was awesome, but the Airbnb cottage we were now in was even better. Set in a secluded location with just two other cabins, it was amazingly spacious inside with a kitchen-diner, modern bathroom, bedroom, and a glorious BBQ grill that we took full advantage of. After a trip to the local grocery store to buy some seasoned pork and veggies, our dinner was the best meal we'd had in days, and it was made all the more fun by grilling it outside. Almost a paradise on earth, but no Northern Lights this time.

Chapter 8

Living an Abundant Life

"There is no reason to ever be ashamed of where you're at. Not when you are doing your best. Not when you are in your best moment. There are always going to be people to tell you no. Or 'You can't.' Or 'You shouldn't.' It is going to happen. No matter what anybody says, you just must still be like, 'I'm still doing this. I am still going to succeed. I'm still going to do my best.' Defy the odds. Why not?" – Jennifer Lopez

Day 7: Kirkjufell, Hellnar, and Reykjavik

It was our final day in Iceland, so we had to cram in as much as possible before we left. We woke up at around five in the morning, had breakfast, and made our way to Kirkjufell. This is a popular location for photographers, even in the winter. Kirkjufell (translates as "Church Mountain") is very impressive to look at, and in the summer you can hike to the top in about 90 minutes. We mainly wanted to see the famous spot with triple waterfalls in front of the mountain.

Next, we headed to the Hellnar sea cliffs, but on our way there we came across some powerful waves along the coast. I was a little afraid to go near them at first because it seemed they might form a tsunami any second, but they were so compelling that we spent a good amount of time there just taking it all in. This was probably my favourite location of the trip, and I'd really like to come back here the next time I'm in Iceland.

Finally, we headed back to Reykjavik. Not too many scenic views on this drive, but you go through the 3.5-mile Hvalfjordur Tunnel, which is exciting. As we approached the end of the tunnel, Ava asked, "Dad, I hear you talk about abundance and living an abundant life all the time. What do you mean by that?"

The Right to An Abundant Life

Like the words "success" and "wealth", the word "abundance" will mean different things to different people. For me, to live an abundant life is to live to the highest standards possible in the areas of your life that you have decided are the most important to you in terms of living a balanced, full, and complete life. What those areas are will be a matter of inward reflection, and of considering your goals and ambitions in life. I have eight areas that I focus on, and these are areas in which I constantly measure myself and continuously set higher standards. I call them my 8 Fs:

- Faith
- Fitness
- Family
- Finance
- Fun
- Friends
- Fact
- Favour

The order in which they're listed is their order of importance, and Ava wanted to know how I justified ranking fitness above family. I had to agree that it sounds controversial, but what it comes down to is that you can only look after others once you have established yourself in a position of strength, and that means looking after yourself first.

Perhaps this is something that is clearer to a diabetic than to others, but if I focus on my own health and fitness, this will ultimately mean that I stand a better chance of avoiding serious illness, keeping me better able to provide for my family. It also means that I'll live longer (with any luck) and therefore I can be with my family for longer. All my Fs are independently important, but all have a symbiotic relationship with one another and interact to form a complete package that works for me and my goals.

I rank finance at No.4 in my 8 Fs, but it's the foundation that will make reaching high standards in the other areas possible. I don't think you can live a complete, healthy, and successful life unless you have enough money to do so. You will need many things if you are to make the most of your talent or your drive to succeed. To have enough time to practise your faith to a high standard, you need to be in a position of not having to work long hours or multiple jobs.

To have high standards in health and fitness, you need money to buy high quality foods and have time to go to the gym or for a run. You'll need money to have good wholesome fun, including travelling and seeing the world. In order to have a career that pays enough to live life to a high standard, you'll most likely require education and a mentor. Having enough money will make everything possible, and not having enough money could mean that some things will not be possible for you. What it comes down to is not doing things with the primary purpose of making money, but to make money to be able to do the things you want to do.

Ava pointed out that when she hears successful people talking on television about their businesses, the impression she gets is that their primary goal above all else is to make money. There can be no denying that this is true in many cases, and it makes me sad. However, judging others changes nothing. There are those who think that having money is the most important thing in the world. There are also those who think it's the second most important thing in the world, and the most important thing to them is to make sure other people know they've got money. Those are their aims, and judging would be hypocritical because a great deal of what I've said to Ava on this trip has been about defining goals and then organising your life to achieve them.

If some people define their goal as having a million times more money than they can possibly spend, well, that's the goal they've chosen. If others define their goal as making sure other people know they have endless wealth by flagrantly displaying it, then that's the goal they've chosen. Of course, considering everything discussed on our trip, I just suggested to Ava that she should take a look at those people and consider if they look happy. Does the goal of making more money appear to bring real happiness?

I've never had those sorts of goals, and I could see no signs of Ava developing them. For most of us, happiness is about having enough; enough to do the things we really want to do, and what those things are is up to us. One of the great things about being human is that asking 1000 people what they want to do will generally get you over 900 different answers. What I want, and perhaps what most of us want, is to have enough money to live an abundant life. Who is going to be satisfied with a little when they are capable of obtaining, using, and enjoying more?

Money is not the root of all evil, it's the love of money that can be harmful. If you see money as a tool with which you can improve other areas of your life, it's the root of great good. Something I'd like people to ask themselves more often is, "If I can do better, why don't I?" In his book, *The Science of Getting Rich*, William Wattle said, "The purpose of nature is the advancement and development of life, and every man should have all that can contribute to the power, elegance, beauty, and richness of life; to be content with less is sinful." As I see it, God's purpose in creating us was not so that we could live an impoverished life, but so we could live an abundant life. Nature only knows abundance. Leave a piece of land uncultivated for a year and see how many plants grow that weren't there a year earlier. We might call many of those plants weeds, but that isn't the point. The point is that nature works to make more.

God rewards obedience with riches. To this day, Solomon is still regarded as the richest person ever to have lived. Job was rewarded with even more riches when he stayed faithful after being tested. It's possible to become rich by making other people's lives a misery – stealing from them, cheating them – but it's also possible to gain riches as the result of doing great work. For most of us, becoming rich will be a by-product of doing what we love and not the reason for doing what we do.

A question that's simple to ask but difficult to answer is: how much money makes you rich? For many, if you have everything you need to live the life you are capable of living, you're rich. Note that it's the life you are *capable* of living, not the life you are *actually* living. There is inside every one of us a natural drive to become the best we can become. It's unfortunate that this drive is ignored or suppressed by some. It's unfortunate because the person who doesn't do everything possible to be the best they can be won't be happy in the end. Just like a flower is at its best in full bloom, we can only be at our best when we live a complete life. Success in life is becoming what you want to be, and you can only become what you want to be by making use of all the things around you. Some of the things you need, like determination, will come from inside you and are thus free, but others, like education, will cost money.

I said to Ava, "You'll need clothes, and they need to be good enough for you to feel confident when seen wearing them. Your home will need to give you a sense of warmth, comfort, and tranquillity, and that's unlikely to come cheap. You'll need to be free from the anxieties that come with not being able to pay your bills. Rest and recreation, like this trip to Iceland, are also necessary, but we're not done yet. You can't live a good interior life without books, and not only do books have to be paid for, but you also need the time to read. The day will come when you have to consider all of these things for your children as well as for you. If you want to give them the kind of start we've tried to give you, you'll need a high level of income. And when all of that is done, there's no better feeling than that of helping others in need, and you can't give to people in need unless you have something to give. It's for all these reasons that I see nothing wrong with wanting to have enough money to do what you want to do to live a full life. For me, the person who doesn't want to live more abundantly is abnormal. So, how to do it?"

A Recipe for More Money

If I had known at Ava's age what I know now... but what's the point of saying that? We know what we know when we know it. Yes, I'd have done certain things differently, but that wasn't how it was and, in any case, the mistakes we make play a major part in making us who we are. If we want to know how to live an abundant life, all the books we need have already been written.

One of the things I know now that I didn't know in my teens is that certain laws exist which, if we follow them, will result in having enough money. They are an essential part of how we live our life. If we don't follow these laws (in a little while I'm going to describe them as a recipe for a successful life), it doesn't matter how hard we work, we will always be scrabbling to have enough money.

There have been lots of studies centred on people who have become rich. They make interesting reading. One of the things they make clear is that financially successful people are in many respects average. They have no more talent or ability than most others. Many of the rich people in my day were college dropouts. Many had average IQs – no worse than other people's, but no better. So how did they become rich? You could, if you wanted, say that it was nothing but luck. The universe smiled on them more than it did on others. If you decide to take that line, you'll have every reason not to make any special effort yourself, because what would be the point? Lady Luck will smile on you, or she won't. Nothing you can do about it. But I don't happen to believe that. I will accept that environment plays a role. You can't expect to get rich if you are one of ten people living in a desert, but if you have rich people in your town, you can get rich too. You don't have to specialise in any particular field. People can have high levels of income in many fields, although it's true that your chances of success will increase if you have a passion for a certain field that makes the most of your natural talents, and the work you do puts you in flow.

Having said all this, Ava wanted to know what I meant by "flow". Flow is a mental state in which a person performing some activity is fully immersed in a feeling of energised focus, full involvement, and enjoyment in the process of the activity. You love doing what you are doing so much that you don't consider it work, but almost recreation. That's flow. As an example, a novelist I know works in one room in his house that's set aside as his office. There's no phone in there. He writes on a laptop, but the laptop is not connected to the internet. The result is that he's not going to be interrupted by phone calls, emails, or social media. When he's writing, he closes his door. Even his granddaughters, who he loves dearly, know that when Grandad's door is closed, no-one is allowed to even knock on it, unless the something they have to say is that the house is on fire. He begins each morning by rereading the last few pages of his work in progress and the notes he always leaves for himself at the end of a session about what is to happen next. Then he simply sinks into the story. He talks to the characters – and they talk back to him. He described what happened when he was writing one of his books, saying, "The protagonist was called Billy. Billy stood over my left shoulder and kept up a running commentary... 'Poppy wouldn't have said that... Don't forget about the anger management... Tell them what my mother said about the man who was supposed to get her into the movies when she was a girl, but got her into bed instead...'" You could say that in a very real sense, Billy wrote that book. Only Billy doesn't exist.

And while all this is going on, he is unaware of anything else. The postman has probably been and gone, but someone else can open the mail. A delivery driver has probably knocked at the door, but unless someone else is there to answer, they'll just have to come back later. I don't think I've ever heard a better example of someone being in the flow. Would that writer consider himself rich? In financial terms, no. He's never had the huge blockbuster runaway success. You may never have heard of him, but he has everything he needs (including those granddaughters). He pays his bills, and he never finds himself worrying about where his next case of red Bordeaux is coming from. I'd call that abundance, and I know for sure that he regards himself as a happy man.

Obtaining enough money to live an abundant life is not dependent on being in a certain field, but depends on following the laws that have already been identified for us. If someone in a similar field to you is living a full life and you are not, you need to ask yourself why. It will be because the other person conducts their business in a certain way and is following the laws.

In response to this, Ava had another query. She said, "But, Dad, I've heard many people say that it takes money to make money."

She's right, people do say that, but I let her know that no-one is ever prevented from gaining wealth through a lack of money. There are more self-made millionaires in the UK than any other kind. Most started with nothing and created their wealth. It's true that once you have money, making more becomes easier because you've already shown yourself how to do it. But no matter what your background, if you follow the laws fully, you can have enough money to live an abundant life.

An Even Playing Field

This was proving to be a subject that raised lots of questions with Ava. "But, Dad, aren't all the areas where one can make a lot of money already saturated?"

My answer to this was to remind her of the universe of abundance. There is and will always be an abundance of opportunities out there. No-one is ever kept in poverty by a shortness of opportunity, although we're not necessarily talking about becoming a billionaire entrepreneur – nice as that idea might be.

I explained, "What we need to pursue is the acquisition of more value, not more valuables. Personal value is the magnet that attracts all good things into our lives. The greater our value, the greater our reward. I have always lived by the motto that if you want more, you need to be worth more. We, therefore, must be in constant search for new ways to increase our value. In my life and work experience, I've found that income will seldom exceed your own personal development. Somebody once said that if you took all the money from the top 1% in the world and divided it equally amongst everyone else, it would soon be back in the pockets of the same top 1%. Why do you think that is? It's because unless you change how you do things, you will always have what you have. In order to have more, you need to become more."

Studies in the US have shown that beyond a given income, having more doesn't increase your happiness. Obviously, the "given amount" is going to vary from person to person, but the only one that matters is the right figure for you. Now, there are many elements at play here, such as the cost of living where you live and what your definition of abundance is, but it demonstrates that stratospheric levels of income aren't required to live a full life.

Your mindset will also be a key driver in your quest for riches. We all have an established set of attitudes which we can describe as our mindset. There are two kinds of mindset – a fixed mindset and a growth mindset – and which we have will determine our chances of becoming rich. People with a fixed mindset believe you either are or are not good at something – it's just who you are. These people think that the number of opportunities out there is limited. People with a growth mindset believe anything is possible, and that anyone can be good at anything because your abilities are entirely due to your actions. This may sound simple, but it's surprisingly deep. A fixed mindset is the most common, and the least desirable, so it's worth understanding and considering what mindset you have and how it's affecting you. For example:

- In a fixed mindset, you believe things just are as they are. You might see someone being "a natural" at something, while you're just "no good" at doing something. Whatever it is, good or bad, you're stuck with your lot in life.
- In a growth mindset, you believe things can always change. Whatever it is, good or bad, it can be changed with dedicated practice. Anyone can be good at anything.

If you have a fixed mindset, any sort of trouble or difficulty is devastating. In your mind, when things go wrong, you're telling yourself, "See? You'll never be great at this. Give up now," and you do whatever you can to hide your flaws by avoiding putting yourself in a position where you believe you might be judged or labelled a failure. You stick with what you know to keep up your confidence. You look inside yourself to find your true passion and purpose, as if this is a hidden inherent thing. The essence of a fixed mindset is that what defines you is your failures. It's all about the outcome. If you fail, you think all effort was wasted. In short, a fixed mindset can only ever hold you back.

A growth mindset is completely different. If you have this, you see trouble as important feedback in the learning process. Your flaws constitute a to-do list of things to improve. You keep up your confidence by always pushing into the unfamiliar, to make sure you are always learning. You commit to mastering valuable skills regardless of mood, knowing that passion and purpose come from doing great work, and not by luck or predestination, but from expertise and experience. In a growth mindset, failures are temporary setbacks. In short, it takes a growth mindset to become your best self in all aspects of life.

Where a fixed mindset is all about the outcome, in a growth mindset, it's all about the process, and outcomes hardly matter. As Gerry Rafferty sang, "If you get it wrong, you'll get it right next time." An important thing to know is that your mindset can be changed; mindsets are not fixed in themselves. If you recognise a fixed mindset attitude in yourself, you can change it by being aware of it and taking steps to change your thinking. Being open to change is all it takes to begin the process of change for the better.

Now, back to that recipe for a successful life.

The Recipe Ingredients

Something that really great cooks know is that recipes, like mindsets, aren't fixed. You have a recipe for a meal you haven't cooked before and it sounds wonderful, but when you look in your kitchen cupboards, you find that one of the recipe's ingredients is the one thing you don't have. If you have a fixed mindset, chances are you'll give up at that point. If you have a growth mindset, it's much more likely that you'll look for what you do have that you could use as a substitute.

Or maybe it's even more straightforward than that. Like the cook who realised she had a lot of leftover Bolognese sauce in the freezer that needed to be used up. She also had some leftover lasagne sheets in the cupboard, so an instant solution was to make lasagne for dinner. However, after thawing the Bolognese sauce, she realised it was in fact leftover beef stew – so what now for dinner? You don't make lasagne with beef stew. Well, just because you don't doesn't mean you can't. In a growth mindset, you give it a try. Maybe it'll be delicious, maybe it won't, but unless you try, you're not going to know.

This is a message that's repeated in so many ways. Sticking with a culinary theme, if you travel to the

Perigord Noir in south-west France, one of the dishes you'll find on most menus is cassoulet. If you try it and enjoy it, you might Google a recipe for it when you get home, and gather the ingredients you need. However, something you should know is that there's no one recipe for cassoulet. Every restaurant serving it has their own take on what ingredients to use. The restaurants in the town of Souillac all serve their own versions, and if you travel a little further to Rocomadour, you'll find other chefs preparing yet more different cassoulet recipes. Visit another town, and you'll begin to realise there are enough cassoulet recipes to fill a book. What this illustrates is that when we talk about a recipe, we don't necessarily mean that every ingredient has to be used exactly as the recipe says. If you don't have one of the called-for ingredients, what *do* you have?

With this said, the first step in this recipe for success is to acknowledge that you are what you think about most. The universe will help manifest what you think about, so you are a product of your thoughts. Nothing has ever existed without first being thought about. Thought is the starting point of all creation. Humans are different from all other living creatures in that we do not live on instinct alone. To have enough money, you need to think and do things a certain way. A person's way of doing things is the direct result of the way they think about things. To do things in the way you want to do them, you have to acquire the ability to think the way you need to think. Everyone has a natural ability to think about whatever they choose to think about, but not everyone can think deeply and specifically about what they really want from life. Odd as it may sound, many people go through life not knowing what they believe in, what they stand for, or what they want from life. What would success really mean for them? How can you go and get what you want, if you don't know exactly what it is you want? The universe can only help you when you have detailed thoughts and specific ideas about what you want. The universe can't help you manifest vague thinking.

The second step is to believe that the universe is your friend and will help you obtain what you think about. It's very important that you have faith in the universe to hear your thoughts and help you manifest them, and one of my favourite quotes comes from Napoleon Hill, who said, "Whatever the mind of man can conceive and believe, the mind of man can achieve." So, first you need to have a thought, then you need to believe or have faith that it can be achieved, and the result of this will be achieving your goals and living an abundant life.

At this point, I said to Ava, "Don't ask me why this is the case, and how this is all possible. I don't know. It's just how it is; how the universe is ordered. Many more people of much more intelligence than me still can't explain the universal science behind this phenomenon, but we know it's there. I guess, just like we can't see the air we breathe but we know it's there, this universal force is out there helping us. I believe that God created us to live an abundant life, and God gave us a recipe for a happy complete life."

Nothing Wrong With Wanting More

When I was young, I used to have this mental block about money, believing that wanting to have money to do things was somehow a bad desire, and staying poor or content with little was what God wanted from us. Bible verses like Mark 10:25, where it states that it's easier for a camel to go through the eye of a needle than for someone rich to enter the kingdom of God, always made me think that being or wanting to be rich is a bad thing. But this is not the case, and I never want Ava to have any notion that it's God's will for her to be poor.

God's desire is that every one of us should live a full life and enjoy all the wonderful things He created for us. God wants us to be *rich* because He can express himself better through us if we have plenty of things that He can use to express himself through. In a modern world where we want to show the glory of God to non-believers, it wouldn't be a good advertisement for the blessings that come from God if all believers are seen to live in poverty.

Humans and all of nature are designed to produce more and to continually increase. One apple seed grows into a tree that produces many apples and many more seeds. The same goes for our mental capacity. We are designed to keep improving – to know more, to do more, and to become more. To do this, you'll need money to make use of all the tools around you, and so it becomes clear that those who have those tools get more. The important thing is not to forget the lesson we've already learned: that the desire for more money should not be for accumulation's sake, but to build the capacity to live a fuller life. The goal is to want a full life, not more pleasure and more things. A full life is not a flashy life. You don't want to have more money solely for mental pleasures, or to get knowledge just to outshine others. You also don't want more money solely to help other people and therefore lose yourself in saving others. You want more money to be able to eat healthy foods, surround yourself with beautiful things, travel to faraway lands, feed your mind and develop your intellect, and help people in need from a position of strength.

I said to Ava, "Always remember that what God wants is for you to make the most of yourself, for you and then for others. You can help others more by making the most of yourself than in any other way."

Let's look at each of the 8 Fs in turn.

Why Faith?

There is a famous quote by Thomas Aquinas: "To one who has faith, no explanation is necessary. To one without faith, no explanation is possible."

By faith, I don't necessarily mean religious faith, even though that is my application of the word. Faith for others might be confidence and belief in something without necessarily having scientific proof. Sometimes, when things don't go according to plan, we lose faith, not only in ourselves but also in any potential outcome in our lives. Failure will do that to you. When we experience life's failures, it's easy to lose hope, and even faith.

Faith and hope are not the same thing. Faith is deep-rooted in the expectation of good things to come. It goes beyond hope. While much of hope lives in the mind, faith is steeped in the heart and the spirit. It can't be explained away by reason or logic, or be understood through a single dimension. While life can be hard at the best of times, faith is the knowledge, deep down inside, that things will get better. It's taking the next step when you can't see the entire staircase. Simply put, in my opinion, life would fail to have reason if we didn't have faith.

We couldn't drive our cars without faith that someone else won't crash into us. If we didn't have faith, how could we fly 35,000 feet above the ground in an aeroplane? Without faith, how could we move from one moment to the next without completely second-guessing everything we did? Without faith, we can't expect things to turn out right for us no matter what the situation might be. Looking at it this way, faith is just as important as the air we breathe. While the oxygen in the air nourishes the body, faith nourishes the heart and the soul. It's the energy that courses through every single fibre and cell in our beings. It's the fundamental foundation of our existence.

People have moved mountains with their faith. Even when situations seemed dire and bleak, it was their faith that carried them through. There is little explanation for it in the physical realm; it is the metaphysical fibre that binds us all, carrying each of our deepest wishes and desires. That's where faith lives. Unfortunately, some people don't believe in things they can't see. They explain things away as being due to other causes and effects, failing to find the small miracles in life that exist and are constantly working in our favour. Having faith in your life is enormously important.

Faith is not just a notion that some people hold onto in tough times; faith is an important element in all human life on earth. Life is precious, but it can also be remarkably difficult at times. Faith helps to get us through, illuminating the pathway in times of darkness, helping to give us strength in times of weakness. Without faith, we are nothing.

Why Fitness?

Edward Stanley once said that those who think they have no time for bodily exercise will sooner or later have to find time for illness. I agree. Remember the airline advice that adults should put on their oxygen masks first before helping children? It's only by looking after yourself that you remain in a position of strength to be able to help others. This still applies when you're on the ground; the difference being that a position of strength now means staying physically fit and healthy rather than wearing an oxygen mask.

We all know that self-care is important to maintain a healthy relationship with yourself. It produces positive feelings, boosts your confidence and self-esteem, and it serves to remind you (as well as others) that you and your needs are worthy of attention. It doesn't matter whether you're a teenager or a grandparent, at any age and stage in life we need regular physical activity. Staying active promotes good health, and understanding the benefits of physical fitness and knowing how active you should be can help improve your overall quality of life. Something William James once said sums this up nicely: "The Lord may forgive us our sins, but our nervous system never does." It's also a question raised in the Bible: What shall it profit a man if he gains the whole world and loses his health?

Chronic disease causes seven out of every 10 deaths. While some diseases can't be prevented, you can reduce your risk of developing certain diseases, including heart disease and Type 2 diabetes, by reducing risky behaviours and living a healthy lifestyle. It's unknown what led to my Type 1 diabetes diagnosis, but making healthy choices and engaging in regular physical activity can reduce the risk of experiencing many health issues and complications. Numerous studies have shown that regular physical activity increases life expectancy and reduces the risk of premature mortality. There is no magic formula that translates hours of physical activity into days of life gained, but research suggests that more active people tend to be healthier and live longer.

Regular exercise and physical activity increase muscle strength, bone density, flexibility, and stability. Studies have also shown that exercise improves your mood and overall mental health. Staying active and healthy allows you to do things that require a certain level of physical fitness. For example, yesterday we hiked to the top of a mountain. It was a rewarding experience and instilled a sense of accomplishment in both of us, but a lack of fitness means there are people to whom those experiences are denied. Of course, you don't need to conquer mountains to feel the rewards. Even just walking around local areas can be a challenge for those who've allowed themselves to become sedentary. It's never too late to become more active, and it should be considered a simple case of "use it or lose it". Being more active today will make it easier to stay active tomorrow and into old age, enjoying fun times with loved ones and creating special memories along the way.

If there is a more precious gift than life, I don't know what it is, so why waste it when we have the choice to live a more meaningful existence? Yes, it's always possible to find an excuse, but taking care of yourself is your responsibility.

Why Family?

Family is an important word. Nietzsche said that in family life, love is the oil that eases friction, the cement that binds together, and the music that brings harmony. It means to feel secure, to have someone you can count on and share problems with, and it also means having respect and taking responsibility for each other. Your parents are the first and most important teachers in your life. The importance of family starts at birth and stays constant throughout life. As you grow into your teens and early adulthood, good parents can and will be a bedrock of support during times of change for you.

Family is about creating strong relationships and providing a sense of meaning and belonging. Families should be a source of unconditional love and a resource for all of us to weather life's changes and challenges. In healthy families, children can learn what it means to be a happily married woman or man, along with the qualities a good father or mother has. Most people would also agree on the importance of family in creating healthy individuals and strong communities. At a basic level, communities are just a group of families, and the healthier the families are, the healthier the community will be.

A family should be a bedrock of encouragement, respect, and love, to help every member thrive. In today's hyper-connected world, it's easy to get over-exposed to unhealthy ideas and images, but a close family with strong values can help young family members avoid or resist negative influences. Without strong family values, young people can succumb to peer pressure and stumble on unwanted consequences.

Families can be one of life's true joys. Whether you have a small, close-knit family like the three of us, or come from a larger family like Ava's cousins, you should be able to turn to your family for strength and support. A loving family can support every member's physical and emotional needs. With positive guidance from their family, each person can set goals and work towards them. Healthy families also recognise each person as an individual, celebrating each family member's unique differences.

Why Finance?

As set out above, your number one goal in terms of living an abundant life will be to have enough money to service all the things you want to do. This was perhaps said best by P.T. Barnum when he commented that money is a terrible master but an excellent servant. This is how you should see money, as a servant.

Sadly, our culture sends out conflicting messages about money. One message is that money is everything, sent out in celebrity culture, the rich and famous, Wall Street greediness, jealousy at the sight of a house bigger than ours, or a car newer than our car. Another message is the complete opposite, sent out in the cultivation of suspicion around wealth and the wealthy, and targeted teaching aimed at telling us not to envy them, to see the limitations of wealth and the potential trouble it causes instead. In some families, it gets to the point of money being a dirty word, not something that should be discussed, and never flaunted because doing so is tacky. In these homes, being poor is almost a virtue.

However, money is important. Whatever we feel about money, people with money, or the pursuit of money, we must agree that money *is* important. Money can be a great helper, but a bad servant. Wealth is not found in having great possessions, but in having few wants. Having few wants is probably the best insurance against greediness, because it's human nature to keep wanting more, and the more you have, the more you want. It's a simple psychological process. You have the basics such as shelter, food, clothes, etc., and you're fairly happy, although you do worry about dealing with emergency situations. You become wealthier, and you enjoy the extra luxuries for a few months, but then it becomes your new normal. Now, surrounded by wealthier people, you look around, and you feel unhappy. They have more than you. You want more. But when you get more, you soon become unhappy again... it's a never-ending cycle.

Money on its own is neither good nor bad, it's a means to an end. This doesn't mean that money is not important. It *is* important, but as a tool that enables you to protect yourself, to build yourself and your family a better life, and to give back to your community. Money is important because when you have it you can't be destitute. Money is important because it enables you to have more control over your life, more freedom to carve out your own path, and fewer constraints on your choices. Money is important because it means fewer financial worries. Sure, the wealthy worry, too – they worry about losing their fortune, for example – but this is not the same as worrying about being able to put food on the table. Money is important because having money means that life is not a constant effort to keep your head above water. Having money enables you to live life to the fullest, enjoy adventures and textures and tastes, and make the most of the 80 or so years you can look forward to. Life is short, and where most like to say you only live once, I say, no, you only die once. You live every day.

Why Facts?

By facts, I mean learning new things and being a lifelong student – to never stop learning. Robin Sharma, one of my favourite authors, believes that investing in yourself is the best investment you will ever make. It will not only improve your life, but also the lives of those around you. I'm always curious about the world, and always aware of how much I can still learn. Personal fulfilment and development refer to natural interests, curiosity, and motivations that lead us to learn new things. For example, the things we learned about Iceland during this trip. What we learn, we learn for ourselves, not for someone else.

Why Fun?

Most of us want to have more fun, but it can seem, at times, not to be as easy as it used to be. The reasons are many. It may be guilt, because others are not having fun; it may be perceived inappropriateness, because others around us can't have fun; or it may be a lack of time, because our commitment to others will not let us have fun. As George Bernard Shaw once said, "We don't stop playing because we grow old; we grow old because we stop playing."

Something we need to remember is that what's fun for one person might not be fun for another. Nevertheless, there can be little doubt that having more fun improves your relationships, both at work or school, and in life in general. Research shows that when we have fun with others, these experiences have a positive effect on building trust and developing communication. Having fun gives us an opportunity to connect and be creative. When we laugh together, this sends an external non-verbal message that says we're alike, and we share values. It can also make us look more vulnerable, but at the same time approachable and friendly, which can help build connections and bonds.

Engaging in enjoyable activities can be an especially powerful antidote to stress. It has been recognised in several studies that spontaneous laughter has a stress-buffering effect that helps us better cope with stress. It has been proven that individuals who laughed less had more negative emotions when compared to those who laughed more. In contrast, those who laughed more showed fewer negative feelings, even when stressful situations increased. Stress is draining. It can suck the life out of us, making us tired and moody, so reducing our stress levels can give us a new boost of vitality. Having fun and playing are traditionally associated with children and the early years of our development, however, many philosophers and psychologists emphasise the importance of play as we get older. Plato professed that life must be lived as play, and I have always said that I want to grow up, but never grow old.

Why Friends?

It was Helen Keller who said that she would rather walk with a friend in the dark than walk alone in the light, and I'd agree with that. Friends can challenge and confuse us, and sometimes we might wonder why we even bother, but friendship is as important to our wellbeing as eating right and exercising. What's more, friendships help us grow through each year of our lives.

The people we bring into our lives as friends will show us how to forgive, laugh, and make conversation. The basic components of any relationship, from school friends to marriage partner and co-workers, are all founded in friendship. We learn how to interact with people because of our friends, even the ones that are opposite from us or share a different worldview. We don't just talk with others, but learn from them. We understand the process of meeting new acquaintances and finding out what makes them tick. These people help push us out of our comfort zone, while still providing a safe emotional space for us to be totally ourselves.

One of the most overlooked benefits of friendship is that it helps keep our minds and bodies strong. I once read an article which concluded that having solid friendships in our life can even help promote brain health. Friends help us deal with stress, make better lifestyle choices that keep us strong, and rebound more quickly from health issues and disease. The same article suggested that spending time with positive friends changes our outlook for the better. We are happier when we choose to spend time with happy people.

Friends don't completely cure loneliness, but they do help us during lonely times. We learn how to accept kindness and to reach out when we need help. Those painful times when we might be without friends also help us to appreciate the friendships that come in and out of our lives. Having a steady stream of friends lets us know that some friendships will not last forever, but each one brings something special. We learn more about ourselves and how important it is to have someone, just one person, who knows and understands us. This is the key to coming out of loneliness.

Good friends can change our value system, so we learn to inject more meaning into our lives. In spending time with good friends, we fill up our lives with great conversation, heartfelt caring and support, and laugh-out-loud fun. When we fall on hard times, friends are there to put things in perspective and help us. When we have success, they are smiling at our good fortune. With down-to-earth, positive people in our life, we will be more mindful of gratitude and doing nice things for others. I believe that when we have healthy friendships, we don't just live, we thrive.

Sometimes building and keeping good friendships can seem like hard work, and it is, because anything worthwhile is always hard work. But great reward comes from hard work.

Why Favour?

The favour I mean here is a favour done with no expectation of getting something in return. This might be anything from taking the rubbish out for your elderly neighbour, buying a meal for a homeless person, volunteering at your favourite charity, or supporting a wildlife fund in Africa through a financial donation. It was Mahatma Gandhi who said that the best way to find yourself is to lose yourself in the service of others.

I believe you'll never regret time spent supporting a cause you're passionate about. It will enrich your life, familiarise you with your community, and connect you to people and ideas that will positively impact your perspective for the rest of your life. Helping your community is an opportunity for you to grow as a person, to better understand how you fit into the world around you, and it sets a great example for younger family members. Spending time enriching your community is a great way to broaden your perceptions of the world. By immersing yourself in a community and surrounding yourself with people dedicated to making the world a better place, you can learn so much about how the world works. You gain a unique sense of purpose by serving those around you, one which often manifests in other areas of your life. Donating your time to support those around you is extremely beneficial, both for you and your community.

When you volunteer, you can meet lots of new people. Working alongside like-minded individuals who also care about improving their surroundings will allow you to broaden your network of friends. Additionally, it will help you to better understand the circumstances of other members of your community. Having a broad, open-minded perspective of the different walks of life around you will help you to be an effective and empathetic citizen. Dedicating your time to help others will teach patience, kindness, and resilience. Not only will you improve your communication abilities by working alongside a diverse team of people, but you will also gain a plethora of other experiences that will help you as you navigate your future. Volunteering may even help you discover a new passion or interest.

There are so many important causes out there that always need volunteers to support the work they are doing. Whatever you are passionate about, you can find a valuable way to donate your time. Many towns and cities have community centres that can be great places to find opportunities to give back in the place you call home. If giving back to the community sounds like a feat reserved for heroes, that's your limiting beliefs doing the talking. The reality is that everyone's life experience is unique, and your set of experiences equips you with skills and a perspective no-one else can duplicate. You don't have to be perfect to give back, all you need is the self-acceptance necessary to embrace everything you have to offer. Not only will your actions benefit those on the receiving end of your good deeds, but you will find a personal sense of joy and fulfilment through your contributions.

The Importance of Being Specific

Something I wanted to make clear to Ava was that it's not enough to have a general desire for wealth "to do good with" – everybody has that desire. It's not enough to wish to travel, see things, and live more – everybody has those desires, too. You need to be much more specific in what it is you want. I said, "Think detail. Imagine if we'd got into this car at the start of our trip and knew nothing more than we wanted to start from Reykjavik and travel east. Who knows where we would have ended up, especially in this country where the elements are so raw? We had to put the exact coordinates into our Sat Nav so that we could have faith we'd end up where we intended to be.

"The same goes for what you ask of the universe. You need to be very specific in what you ask for. Being specific is usually the most difficult part for people. To know themselves, and to know exactly what they want from life. To be happy is a noble desire, but of little use. You need to see clearly in your mind what it is that will make you happy. What are your goals in the short term? Where do you see yourself in five years? In 20 years? Take your time and think these steps through properly, and then write them down.'

I suggested rating herself against each of the 8Fs, and setting goals within each of them. When this is done regularly, perhaps monthly, trends can be spotted and areas where you're doing well or areas that need focus identified. You can't improve what you don't measure, and you can't measure anything without being specific about what it is you want to measure.

Once you have a clear picture of what it is you want, the next thing is to have a strong desire to achieve it. The clearer and more definite you make your goals, the more you dwell on them, and by thinking of the specifics, the stronger your desire will be. I said to Ava, "The stronger your desire, the easier it will be for you to hold your mind fixed on the goals you want to achieve. Without purpose and desire, your goals are nothing but dreams, and you don't want to be just a dreamer."

Keeping Your Thoughts Focused

Belief and desire are what make your dreams come true. What will help you to keep this faith is guarding your thoughts. Your desire will be shaped by everything you observe and think about. If you want to become rich, you can't think about being poor. Thoughts can't be manifested by thinking about their opposites. I'm not saying that you should be cold-hearted or unkind, but you can never have what you want by being influenced by its opposite. If you want to help the poor, getting rich is the only real way to do so. You can't hold steady in your mind the image of wealth if you fill your mind with images of poverty as well. Don't watch or read anything that fills your mind with images of poverty or suffering. You can't help the poor by learning more about the poor. I believe that what helps people get more from life is showing them images of what an abundant life can look like. The poor don't need more charity; they need more inspiration. Why not inspire people around you through your actions? Show them that if you could do it, so can they.

Also, remember that a strong person can't help a weaker person unless the weaker person is willing to be helped. Even then, the weaker person must become strong themselves. They must by their own efforts develop the strength they admire in another. Only they can alter their condition. Stay focused wholly on your goal to have enough money, and ignore poverty. Use positive language. Whenever you think or speak about those who are poor, think and speak about them as those who are becoming rich.

Only Applied Knowledge Is Power

Even though no riches will ever be manifested without thinking about them, the belief that you can have what you want must be focused on in detailed desire for it. You must act. You must turn your wish or dream into reality, and that can only happen through action. It isn't true that knowledge is power; only *applied* knowledge is ever power.

I said to Ava, "By thought, the thing you want is brought to you, by action you receive it. Put your whole mind into present action, not future action, because the future is never guaranteed. Take action now. There is never any time but now, and there never will be any time but now." To help her put this into context, I added, "Say you're 48 years old and you're scared to start a four-year course because by the time you finish, you'll be 52. Well, guess what. Whether you take the course or not, in four years' time you'll still be 52, so why not be 52 doing something you love? But you need to take action now."

Some of your actions will lead to successful results and some will lead to failure. No-one's actions will *always* lead to success. The key is to never stop taking action. Even when you're afraid, nervous, and anxious about what the consequences of your actions might be, you need to take action. Remember that taking no action is still taking action, but usually with undesired outcomes. Indecision is the thief of opportunity. It will steal your chances for a better future. Fear will try to keep you in your comfort zone, but it's only outside your comfort zone that magic happens. Outside the comfort zone is where you will grow. Fear is enemy No.1 to success; fear stops people from capitalising on opportunity; fear weighs you down, as fear is a powerful force.

In Summary

Our trip is almost over, and we've covered a lot of ground in every sense of the word, so now seemed like a good time to remember the main points we'd discussed. In summary, they were:

- You can get and become whatever you put your mind to.
- Everything ever created started with a thought, and you need to think about what it is you want.
- You need to believe and show faith in the power of the universe and that it will help you manifest your thoughts.
- You need a strong desire to reach your goals, because without it you won't persist in their pursuit.
- Your goals should not be vague; you need to be specific in terms of exactly what it is you want.
- Stay focused on what you want, and don't let negative thoughts distract you from what you want.
- And lastly, it's important to take action today. You'll make mistakes along the way; learn from them and never stop moving forward through taking action.

"Ava, my hope for you is that you will never be satisfied. I hope you will constantly feel the urge to improve and set higher standards, not only for yourself, but for the world around you. From now on, the end result is all that matters. If you follow this simple recipe in all parts of your life, you will be well on your way to becoming awesome."

Final Thoughts on Our Final Day

It's three in the afternoon and the few rays of sun have all but disappeared. Approaching Reykjavik, where we'll spend our last night before an early departure in the morning, I find myself thinking what a wonderful experience this trip has been for me.

It was just what the doctor would have ordered, had I consulted him. What a beautiful country Iceland is. It's still my favourite country to visit, and I'll come back again and again. There are just so many spectacular landscapes on this island where you feel like you are on a different planet, but most of all, I enjoyed the quality time I spent with Ava.

At 14 years old, Ava is at the very start of her life's journey. I know that she can become whatever she puts her mind to. She has inherited her mother's stubbornness, and I believe that will serve her well in her pursuit of her goals. I loved our conversations during the trip, and think that I have also learned more about myself.

Thank you, Iceland, for another great adventure. You made me find myself again. You made me draw close to my daughter again. Thanks to you Iceland, Ava now has all the tools needed to aspire for abundance.

The End

Bibliography

As A Man Thinketh – James Allen – 1903;
Awaken The Giant Within – Tony Robbins – 1991;
Big Magic – Elizabeth Gilbert – 2015;
Don't Sweat The Small Stuff – Richard Carlson – 1997;
Eat That Frog – Brian Tracy – 2001;
Ego Is The Enemy – Ryan Holiday – 2016;
Emotional Intelligence – Daniel Coleman – 1995;
First Things First – Stephen R. Covey – 1994;
Flow – Mihaly Csikszentmihalyi – 1990;
High Performance Habits – Brendan Burchard – 2017;
How To Stop Worrying And Start Living – Dale Carnegie – 1948;
How To Be A Stoic – Massimo Pigliucci – 2017;
How To Win Friends And Influence People – Dale Carnegie – 1936;
How Successful People Think – John C. Maxwell - 2003;
How To Get Rich – Felix Dennis – 2006;
In Tune With The Infinite – Ralph Waldo Trine – 1897;
Meditations – Marcus Aurelius – AD161;
Mindset – Carol S. Dweck - 2006;
Rich Dad, Poor Dad – Robert T. Kiyosaki – 1997;
Success Through A Positive Mental Attitude – Napoleon Hill – 1959;
The 5AM Club – Robin Sharma – 2018;

The Seven Habits of Highly Effective People – Stephen R. Covey – 1989;

The Book – Alan Watts – 1966;

The Dynamic Laws of Prosperity – Catherine Ponder – 1962;

The Game of Life and How To Play It – Florence Scovel Shinn - 1925;

The Magic of Thinking Big – David J. Schwartz – 1959;

The Motivational Manifesto – Brendan Burchard – 2014;

The Path of Prosperity – James Allen – 1901;

The Power of Positive Thinking – Normal Vincent Peale – 1952;

The Prophet – Kahlil Gibran – 1923;

The Purpose Driven Life – Rick Warren – 2002;

The Power Of Habit – Charles Duhigg - 2012;

The Secret – Rhonda Byrne – 2006;

The Success Principles – Jack Canfield – 2004;

The Greatest Salesman In The World – Og Mandino – 1968;

The Science of Getting Rich – Wallace D. Wattles - 1910;

The Wisdom of Life – Arthur Schopenhauer – 1851;

Think And Grow Rich – Napoleon Hill – 1937;

Blog - Thirteen Truths of Being Thirteen – Elease Colcord – 2017;

Your Invisible Power – Genevieve Behrend – 1921;

"You Are Awesome" (Poem) – Ariadne Brill – 2012.

Copyright Acknowledgement

Every reasonable effort has been made to trace copyright holders, but if there are any errors or omissions, Robert Jacobs will be pleased to insert the appropriate acknowledgments in any subsequent printings and additions. You can contact Robert at feedback@aspireforabundance.co.uk

"Ava, go on, take on this whole world. But to us you know you'll always be our little girl."

Mom & Dad

2021 - Ava, aged 7 & Mama, aged *

Aspire for Abundance Reflection Notes...

Aspire for Abundance Reflection Notes...

Aspire for Abundance Reflection Notes...

Lightning Source UK Ltd.
Milton Keynes UK
UKHW010749200522
403294UK00001B/162